EXERCISES
IN
ELEMENTARY COUNTERPOINT

BY

PERCY GOETSCHIUS, Mus. Doc.

(Royal Württemburg Professor)

*Author of "The Material used in Musical Composition," "The Theory
and Practice of Tone-Relations," "The Homophonic Forms of
Musical Composition," "Models of the Principal
Music Forms," "Exercises in Melody-
Writing," "Applied Counterpoint,"
"Lessons in Music
Form," etc.*

Seventh Edition

G. SCHIRMER, INC., NEW YORK

PREFACE.

THE present volume is intended and expected to cover more ground than its title implies.

In the author's mind it represents a course in Harmony, quite as much as in Counterpoint.

It owes its inception to the author's often expressed conviction that these two courses of study cannot be separated; and also to a constantly strengthening belief that the most rational, quickest and best way to acquire a thorough knowledge of the chords and their uses (the recognized purpose of the study of Harmony) is to begin with one part, to pass from that to two, from that to three, and thus gradually arrive at full four-part harmony.

For this reason, an extensive preparatory knowledge of Harmony is not at all necessary, though a *general* knowledge of the chords will facilitate the study of this book, and is therefore recommended.

Such general familiarity may be gained by the study of Part II of my " Material," or Chapters III to XXX of my " Tone Relations."

*　　*　　*

The full four-part texture, when approached in this way, as systematized in these chapters, will have developed itself naturally into " Counterpoint "; and its acquisition will fully prepare the student to undertake the subsequent tasks in homophonic and polyphonic composition.

THE AUTHOR.

NEW YORK, February, 1910.

TABLE OF CONTENTS.

EXERCISES IN
ELEMENTARY COUNTERPOINT

INTRODUCTION.

Music, theoretically considered, consists altogether of LINES OF TONE. It more nearly resembles a picture, or an architectural drawing, than any other art-creation; the difference being that in the drawing the lines are visible and constant, while in music they are audible and in motion. The separate tones are the points through which the lines are drawn; and the impression which is intended, and which is apprehended by the intelligent listener, is not that of single tones, but of *continuous Lines of tones*, describing movements, curves and angles, rising, falling, poising, — directly analogous to the linear impressions conveyed by a picture or drawing. The popular name for such a tone-line is "Melody." As several tone-lines are usually being traced simultaneously, it follows that several corresponding melodies may, and generally do, appear together. The term Melody, however, is applied specifically to the principal, or most prominent line.

When a number of tone-lines are intonated together, it is evident that they should agree, or harmonize with each other. The process by which this agreement is assured is commonly known as "Harmony."

*   *   *

Tones are associated in two different ways: First, in vertical columns, or *simultaneously*, in solid bodies of tone, usually known as Chords; and second, in lateral order, or *successively*, in strands of tone which we shall call Tone-lines, or melodies. For example, the tones *c-e-g*, arranged vertically, give a chord-body, or harmony, each separate tone of which may be a point in some tone-line (Ex. 1, *a*). The same tones, arranged successively, give a tone-line or melody (Ex. 1, *b*):

a. Chord.   *b.* Tone-line.

Ex. 1.

It is of the utmost importance that the music student should adopt and cultivate the habit of apprehending music according to this definition, as a *System of Lines*. The beginner, and the ordinary hearer, are inclined to regard music merely as a series of chords, a succession of

1

tone-groups, and to associate mentally only those tones that are sounded together (simultaneously, as Ex. 1, *a*). This is surely a natural view, and correct as far as it goes, for the harmonic basis of all music is unquestionably the chord. But it is an imperfect view. The object of the chords is, simply, to fix (approximately) the points through which the lines run ; and unless these *lines* are grasped and traced, — unless the hearer can associate mentally the tones that *follow* each other, the true purpose and significance of the whole tone-association is missed. This must be so, because the only evidence of Life in music lies in the motions which interlink the tones in flowing lines ; and these lines are, therefore, the only tangible element in the art of tone.

The real musical picture then, is a delineation ; an image of sounding and moving lines. Quite aside, for the present, from the numerous qualities which enter into these lines, — their directions, their speed, their rhythm (freedom and variety of changing motions), their spaces, and even their indefinable sensuous or spiritual attributes, — the fundamental fact must be grasped that it is these lines which create the musical impression. The "music" lies in its melodies. Music *is* "tone-lines" ; and the quality of the several lines determines the quality of the composition ; the vitality of the lines equals the life in the music ; and the degree of harmony which governs the association of the lines fixes the euphonious standard of the composition, — its pleasurable effect upon the natural sense of harmony or concord.

*   *   *

To illustrate more fully what is meant by apprehending music as a fabric of tone-strands, tone-lines, or associated melodies, traced, not vertically through the separate chord-forms, but continuously (laterally) from chord to chord, — let us take a passage, at random, from a **Beethoven** Sonata.   In this passage, the master, though certainly guided by his vertical chords, was quite as surely impelled to trace a good, distinctly melodious, effective *tone-line* in each separate part or register : —

The total result, obtained by weaving these four different strands of tone into one compact body (as it came from Beethoven's hand) is as follows : —

Ex. 3.

The music proceeded out of the chords, of course, but the "Music" itself manifests its finished beauty and life and meaning in the Lines of tone. The chords were the means, the lines were the object, of the musical thought. The above musical image (Ex. 3) should therefore appeal to the finer sense of the listener in the forms noted in Ex. 2. He should apprehend each line separately, first of all; and the total sensuous impression should be gained by mentally combining these lines.

* * *

The tone-lines differ greatly in their length, and in the manner of their presentation. Some lines are long, others are often very brief. Sometimes the line is continuous in sound (*legato*), and again it may be intermittent (*staccato*). In the latter case, which is very common, the inner ear of the listener traces the complete line across the silent gaps, just as the eye traces a dotted line as readily as an unbroken one.

Through the following convenient (and customary) method of notation, and its corresponding performance on the pianoforte : —

CHOPIN.

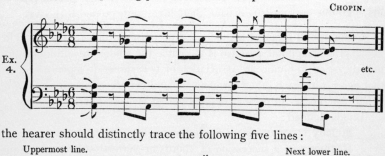

Ex. 4.

etc.

the hearer should distinctly trace the following five lines :

Uppermost line.   Next lower line.

Ex. 5.

The student should carefully examine brief passages from the master-works, with a view to resolving the given bulk into its component lines, as shown in the above examples.   In many cases, only one single prominent line (the "tune" proper, in the uppermost part) seems to be distinctly melodious, — as for instance, in No. 37 of **Mendelssohn's** "Songs without Words."   In others, at least two independent lines are discernible; in a few, the entire bulk may be divided into distinct melodies, — as in the Inventions and Fugues of **Bach**, and many passages in string-quartets, or symphonic scores (where the lines are written separately, of necessity, on independent staves).   In many, finally, the bulk is very uneven, as if, here and there, single extra tones, or brief little lines, had been inserted among the more important, longer melodies.

*   *   *

To some extent, this principle of simultaneous melodies is present in every grade, even the simplest, of music.   It is impossible to connect chords, as, for example, in a hymn-tune, or in the earliest harmony exercises, without tracing such tone-lines.

In four-voice harmony there are four, — known in vocal writing, and familiar to the student (in church choirs or choral societies) as the soprano, alto, tenor and bass.   As a rule, so much preference is given to the uppermost of these (the soprano), that the other singers scarcely realize, themselves, that they too are intoning "melodies" quite as surely as the soprano.

*   *   *

Counterpoint is one of the technical processes of music writing.   The object of contrapuntal practice is to enable the student to add melody to melody, — or to obtain an association of two, three, or more tone-lines that agree with each other harmonically and yet are sufficiently independent of each other to present really different melodic lines.

Briefly defined :

Melody is a succession, or continuous line, of single tones.

Harmony is a succession of chords or vertical columns of tones which harmonize in their simultaneous presentation.

Counterpoint is the harmonious association of individually perfect, but independent, melodies.

CHAPTER I.

THE SINGLE MELODIC LINE.

1. Counterpoint is associated melodies. In good counterpoint, the association is, in a general sense, harmonious, — that is, reasonably accordant, and each melody is good, by itself.

2. Probably the latter condition is the most important. The first consideration, for the beginner, is the correctness of each separate melodic line, independently of the other, or others. Each line, sung or played *alone*, must produce a satisfactory melodic impression.

3. Therefore, the first point to be mastered by the student of harmony, or counterpoint, is the fundamental principle of good melodic movement. He must acquire the ability to judge the quality of a melodic line, and to avoid any tone-progression which is unnatural, — that is, which violates the natural conditions of Melody (smooth, rational, congruous, well-balanced and interesting tone-succession).

4. Should the student harbor any doubt of the existence of laws that govern Melody, or of the possibility of distinguishing good melodies from inferior ones with scientific accuracy, let him compare the following :

with those shown in **Ex.** 2, or with any other examples in this book that are given as specimens of correct, sensible melody.

5. It is not possible, in this necessarily condensed form, to state all of the conditions which enter into the process of perfect melodic formation, a process which is ultimately subtle, and no doubt partly incalculable. But a few general rules may be given, and these the beginner must carefully observe and follow, until his instinct and experience shall enable him to control the finer and finest movements.

6. Probably the most vital law of melody is that which is grounded in the relations and interactions of the primary harmonies of the key, and which determines the *direction of certain Scale-steps.*

Rule 1. The natural or inherent bent of certain Scale-steps must be respected, as far as is possible without monotony. These tendencies are as follows :

The 7th step of the scale moves (naturally) upward.

The 6th and 4th steps of the scale both move (naturally) downward.

7. These are called the Active scale-steps. Their movement extends, generally, only one step; that is:

Step 7 moves to step 8,

Step 6 moves to step 5, and

Step 4 moves to step 3, as a rule,

though wider movements in the proper direction are possible.

For example, in C major:

The other scale-steps (1, 3, 5 and 2) have no such tendencies, and are free to move in any direction, — that is, free as far as *direction* is concerned.

8. When the active tones of the scale move one step, as here shown, they are "resolved"; that is, their active tendencies are gratified, and their movement is finished. But it is always correct, when less decisive movement is desired, for each active step to move two steps at once, or, in other words, to leap a third, — in the proper direction, of course. Thus (C major):

9. To this fundamental rule there is one important exception:

Rule 2. The natural tendency of each active step may be overcome, so that it will move along the scale in the opposite direction, by approaching it (so to speak, by "pushing" it) from the other side, along the scale. Thus, step 7, if preceded by step 8, may pass *on down* to step 6; step 6, preceded by 5, may pass *on up* to step 7; and step 4, preceded by 3, may pass *on up* to step 5.

In other words, the progressions 8-7-6-5, 5-6-7-8 and 3-4-5 are good. Thus (C major):

10. Observe that the successions 7-6-7, 6-7-6, and 5-4-5, cannot be justified in this manner, and should therefore be avoided, for the present. Thus (C major):

EXERCISE I.

THE SCALE-LINE, AND NARROW LEAPS.

The aim of this first lesson is to impress these fundamental melodic movements upon the student's mind, and *habituate* him to them (in case his studies, hitherto, have left this most important work unaccomplished). Therefore, he is required to write a very large number of original melodies, in all the major keys, strictly according to the following directions :

1. At present, only in major.

2. Use chiefly the regular resolutions of the active steps, as shown in Exs. 7 and 8. But do not neglect the irregular movements (Ex. 9).

3. At no point should the melody leap more than a third. All wider skips must be deferred until the next lesson.

4. Any tone may be repeated, anywhere. See par. 20.

5. Use all the simpler kinds of measure (from $\frac{2}{4}$ to $\frac{6}{8}$). The notes may be of uniform rhythmic value, or of different lengths. *See pars. 21, 22 and 23.*

6. The length of the melodies is optional, but it is advisable to write in the regular forms of four or eight measures, closing with the keynote.
For illustration :

CHAPTER II.

WIDER LEAPS.

11. The leap of a third (called a narrow leap), used in the first lesson, is always good. But all wider leaps are generally hazardous, and require specific limitations. The principal consideration is as follows:

Rule 3. Any wide skip is natural, and permissible, when both tones belong to the same good chord.

12. The "good" chords are the primary triads on scale-steps I, V, IV; also the II, though more rare; also the chords of the Dominant-7th and Dominant-9th. The chords on steps VI and III, and all subordinate dissonant chords, are too inferior to afford justification for wide leaps. Thus, in C major:

13. The following wide leaps are therefore good, in either direction:

The following are unnatural, in either direction, and must be avoided, at present:

14. Rule 4. Two or more leaps *in the same direction*, whether narrow or wide, are also strictly subject to this rule: *All* the tones must belong to the same good chord. Thus, C major:

a. All good.

The following are faulty:

Ex. 16.   etc.

NOTE. In the first group, the first skip (*c* to *g*) represents the I, but the next tone, reached with a leap in the *same direction*, does not belong to that (same) chord. The leaping tones, arranged in such a manner, *always remain in the ear*, — " add up," so to speak, — and give the impression of a complete tone-body. The above measures sound thus :

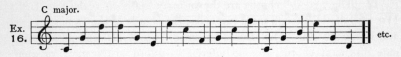

etc.

15. This rule applies only to successive skips in the *same direction*. The moment the direction changes, the ear ceases to " add up " the tones, and judges each leap separately, according to Rule 3. All the faulty progressions of Ex. 16 can therefore be made good *by altering the direction*. Thus :

All good.

Ex. 17.   etc.

16. Rule 5. After a *wide* leap (beyond a third), the melody usually turns, — changes its direction. Thus :

17. Notice, particularly, that this is not obligatory *when the chord remains unchanged*. This is distinctly shown in Ex. 15.

It is generally better to turn, however, after a *wide* leap, even in the same chord; and it is usually quite necessary when the chord changes, — as seen in Ex. 16 (all rectified in Ex. 17). Exceptions do occur, however; see Ex. 20.

18. Rule 6. A skip of *any width* may be made *towards* (or opposite to) the resolving movement of an active scale-step. That is, the resolution of step 7 being upward, any leap *down* to it is correct. And, similarly, any skip may be made *up* to steps 6 and 4. In each case, the melody, in turning after the leap, properly resolves the active step. The following movements are all good (C major):

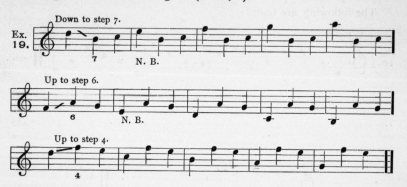

In the measures marked N. B., an exception to a part of Ex. 14 is seen, — skips apparently representing inferior chords. When properly resolved, these progressions are perfectly good.

19. If a wide skip is made, along a good chord-line, contrary to Rule 6, — *up* to 7, or *down* to 6 or 4, — an exception is unavoidable. Either the melody cannot turn, after the wide leap, or the active tone cannot be resolved. Thus:

It is usually better to respect the fundamental law (Rule 1), and resolve the active step properly. Therefore, groups 1, 3 and 5 are better than groups 2, 4 and 6, in the above example.

20. Rule 7. The repetition of a tone, or the octave-leap, is always good:

21. Uniform rhythm is always safe, and generally predominates in a melody. But it incurs monotony, and, therefore, notes of various time-values are effective. At least occasionally, a note of greater value, or of less value than the prescribed beat, should be used.

22. Rule 8. The rhythm is *regular*, and always good, when the *longer* (heavier) tones appear upon the *accented* (heavier) beats, and the *shorter* (lighter) ones upon *unaccented* beats or fractions of beats. Thus, in regular rhythm:

23. If the order is reversed,— if heavy notes occupy light beats, or light notes occupy heavy beats, — the rhythm is *irregular*, and the result doubtful. Still, irregular rhythms may always be rectified by *recurrence*, — that is, by being repeated in the next measure, or some other *corresponding* measure. Thus (both from **Schubert**):

EXERCISE 2.

WIDER LEAPS.

Write, as before, a very large number of original melodies, employing the material of this chapter. Review the directions given in Exercise 1, and follow all but No. 3.

CHAPTER III.

EXCEPTIONAL PROGRESSIONS. MINOR MODE.

24. After thorough exercise of the basic principles of melodic movement, the student will better understand certain less regular traits that may appear in tone-lines. These, though peculiar, and rare, may be fully justified by the circumstances that attend them. A few are specially noted below, and should be thoroughly tested; first at the piano; then with the voice; then with the eye; always with close *mental* application and unceasing reference to the keynote, — *of which the mental ear must always be distinctly conscious.*

25. First, with reference to scale-step 7 (C major):

Explanation. Groups 1, 2 and 3 are good, because step 7 passes *soon* up into step 8. Group 4 is not good, because the skip represents an inferior chord; group 13 is similar, but worse. Group 5 is doubtful, because step 7 does not reach step 8 at all; group 6 is better, because the first three tones represent the Dom.-7th chord, and the resolution of the last one (step 4) satisfies the ear. Groups 7 to 10 are all doubtful, because step 7 makes an extreme leap in the wrong direction; group 10 is the least objectionable, because step 7 recovers itself and ascends to step 8. Group 11 is particularly poor and should be avoided; it may, it is true, occur in the line of the Dom.-7th chord; but step 7 leaps in the wrong direction; it is an awkward leap (augmented fourth), and, landing on step 4, it cannot recover itself. Group 12, on the contrary, is all right, — see Ex. 19, group 13. Group 14 is considered good, — see Ex. 19, group 2. Group 15 appears to violate par. 10; it is permissible, however, because the succession 7-6-7 appears as *embellishment* only, and not as *essential melodic movement.*

26. Second, with reference to scale-step 6:

11. Good. 12. Good. 13. Good. 14. Good. 15. Good.

Explanation. Groups 1, 2 and 3 are good, because step 6 reaches step 5 soon enough. Group 4 is poor, because step 4 is not resolved; group 6 is good; and in group 5, both tendencies are satisfied. Group 7 contains too many irregularities; group 8 is better, — like group 5. Groups 9 and 10 represent an inferior chord. Groups 11 and 12 are justified by Ex. 19. Groups 13 and 14 seem to be adjusted by the resolution of step 7. Group 15 is right, for the reasons given in Ex. 24, group 15, which review.

27. Third, with reference to scale-step 4 :

Ex. 26.

1. Good. 2. Good. 3. Good. 4. ? 5. ?

6. Good. 7. ? ? 8. Good. 9. ? ? 10. ? ? ?

Explanation. Groups 4 and 5 are doubtful, because step 4 ascends and does not return to step 3; compare groups 2 and 6. Group 7 is too irregular. Group 9 has the bad leap from 7 to 3; see Ex. 14, No. 2, and Ex. 24, No. 13. Group 10 is very poor, like Ex. 24, No. 11, and for similar reasons.

28. Rule 9. One of the most vital traits (possibly the supreme one) of good, effective, comprehensible and significant melody, is the arrangement of the tones *in uniform or similar groups or figures.* Thus, a figure (usually a half-measure, whole measure, or two measures in length) may be reproduced as repetition, sequence, or some other closely corresponding form, — generally in some corresponding rhythmic group. For example :

BEETHOVEN.

Ex. 27.

Observe the similarity of formation in the two figures marked *a ;* the second measure is a *sequence* of the first. Also the agreement of *b* and *b.* Also the general resemblance between figures *a* and *b.* Also the slight intentional differences, — *exact* agreement being by no means necessary.

See also Ex. 13, *b* ; Ex. 21 ; Ex. 23, *b.*

29. Such syntactic agreement (uniformity of delineation), *if perfectly distinct*, is often a sufficient excuse for certain irregularities of progression. For example:

In No. 1, the poor progressions 7-6-7 and 5-4-5 are both justified by being sequences of the first measure (which is a blameless figure). In No. 2, the awkward movement from 4 up to 7 is justified by the repetition of the first figure. In No. 3, several poor successions are palliated, as sequences of the very first one,— which is a perfectly good figure.

*　　*　　*

THE MINOR MODE.

30. The harmonic minor scale is derived from the major, by lowering the 3rd and 6th scale-steps of the latter. C minor corresponds to C major, but has *e-flat* and *a-flat*, instead of *e* and *a*. Comp. Ex. 29 with the scale of C major.

Every rule given above applies to minor precisely as to major. That is, the rules which govern C major also govern *C minor* (not A minor), — with one single exception, as follows:

Rule 10. The movement from step 7 to 6, and reversed, from 6 to 7, gives rise *in minor* to an awkward interval (augmented second) which it is better to avoid. Thus, in the so-called " harmonic " or true form of the minor scale:

31. These progressions, from 6 to 7, and from 7 to 6, are, in themselves, justified by Rule 2, Ex. 9. But they must be avoided if the minor scale is to be " melodious " (singable).

32. The remedy is simple, and very common, and consists in so
"altering" the active step as to remove the unmelodious augmented interval. Namely, in passing down from 7 to 6 (in the group 8-7-6-5 only),
lower the 7th scale-step, by an accidental; and in passing up from 6 to 7
(in the group 5-6-7-8 only), *raise the 6th scale-step.* This results in good
singable intervals, and changes the harmonic form to the so-called "melodic" form of the minor scale. Thus:

Ex. 30.

See Ex. 42.

Otherwise, as stated, every melodic condition in major is absolutely valid
for minor.

EXERCISE 3.

EXCEPTIONAL MOVEMENTS, AND THE MINOR MODE.

a. First review every one of the given examples that is in C major, *transposing
each one to C minor* (first at the piano, then with the voice, then with the eye; always
with close mental application).

b. Then transpose every original melody of Exercises 1 and 2 to the corresponding minor mode (that of the *same keynote*).

c. Also write a very large number of original melodies, in major and minor,
applying the principles of this chapter. Before doing this, examine very carefully the
melodies given in Exercises 4, 5, 6, and so forth.

All these original melodies may be used in the coming lessons.

CHAPTER IV.

THE ASSOCIATION OF TWO MELODIC LINES.

33. The principle which naturally governs the association of melodies is that of harmonious agreement. The condition of consonance
should prevail; not to the exclusion of dissonance (as will be seen in a
later lesson), for the latter, in its proper place and proportion, is precisely
as necessary and important in music as consonance. But consonance
should predominate sufficiently to create the impression of "harmonious
agreement" as the ruling condition.

34. The contrapuntal structure — the association of melodies — is
generally obtained in the following manner: some single melody is adopted

as leading part — in a sense, as basis or principal melody (though it must never be forgotten that, in true counterpoint, the melodies are to be of equal value and significance, associated upon an equal footing). To this melody another tone-line is added, by careful adjustment of each of its successive tones to each successive tone of the first melody, in keeping with the simple regulations of harmonious union. In other words, for each tone of the given melody, a tone is chosen that will blend or harmonize consonantly with it, so that the new melody which results will agree, *tone for tone*, with the former. The new melody is therefore in a peculiar sense a product out of the original one, obtained, not by deduction or evolution from within, but by adjustment to it from without.

35. It is quite as correct, however, to create both melodies together, at once, letting each in turn suggest the next melodic move to be made, and making each thus alternately dependent upon the other. This is what the composer no doubt unconsciously does, ultimately. The student will use both processes, but should adopt the former (working with, or "against," a given complete melody) for the present.

36. Rule 1. The " harmonious " intervals, those that are invariably consonant and therefore acceptable for the union of two melodies, are

the THIRD (or tenth), major and minor;

the SIXTH, major and minor ; and

the OCTAVE (or unison), perfect, of course. If, for example, C is given, as lower tone, we may add to it either E, its third ; or A, its sixth ; or C, its octave. If D is given, either F, B, or D, will properly counterpoint it. And so forth. For illustration :

If C is given as upper tone, either A, E, or C may be added to it below ; and the same rule applies to all other tones. Thus :

37. These three intervals are unquestionably permissible at any single point of contact, and the task of the beginner consists simply in determining which of the three is the best at the moment.

38. This choice depends partly upon the *melodic* movement, — for it must be remembered that each part, the given one and the added one, must describe a faultless melodic line (see par. 44). But it also depends partly upon the underlying *harmonic* result, — for the implied chord-successions must also be natural and rational.

39. For illustration of this harmonic distinction : — If the tone C is given, either in the upper or the lower melody (in C major), the 3rd above (and 6th below) will produce the Tonic harmony. The 6th above (and 3rd below) will represent the Subdominant chord, or, possibly, the VI. The 8ve and unison exert no positive influence on the harmony, and become therefore solely a question of *melodic* preference.

Thus :

NOTE. For the rules of good chord-succession, see the author's "Tone-Relations." Or glance at pars. 169 to 176.

40. Whether the *major or minor* form of the 3rd, 10th, or 6th is to be chosen, depends merely upon the *key*, and therefore takes care of itself.

NOTE 1. The distinction between 3rd and 10th, and between octave and unison, may hereafter be dropped altogether, because they are identical.

NOTE 2. In the first lessons, the rhythmic form of the two associated melody-lines will exactly (or nearly) correspond ; that is, each separate note in the given part will have its companion, or "counterpoint," in the added part. An *occasional* exception to this adopted rhythmic scheme may be permitted for good melodic reasons. See Ex. 39, *c*.

41. If the interval 8 (octave) is applied to each successive tone of a given melody, the result is as follows :

Added melody.

The agreement of the added melody with the one that was given, is complete ; the harmony of the association is absolute. But the student perceives at once that here some vital condition is wanting, for by this process nothing more has been obtained than an exact duplication of the given melody. No *new* melody has been produced, and therefore this cannot be called an association of different melodies.

42. The result is more ample if the interval 3, or the interval 6, is used with each of the given tones.   Thus:

But even here, though a new series of tones is produced in each case, it is evident that the added melody is but little more, after all, than a reflection of the given one; an almost exact duplication; precisely the same tone-line, and therefore practically the same melodic product, merely shifted to other steps of the scale.   As true counterpoint is to be no such artless multiplication of one and the same melodic line, but the harmonious association of *independent and individually perfect* melodies, the following rule must be observed:

43. **Rule 2.** In order to secure the independence of the added melody, the interval of the 8ve must be limited to single points, and not be used twice in immediate succession.   The interval of the 3rd (and also that of the 6th) may appear consecutively, but never throughout the entire phrase, and, as a rule, not oftener than three (or four) times in direct succession.   The best result is evidently to be achieved by a sensible interchange of these three different consonant intervals.   Thus, as applied to the above given melody:

44. **Rule 3.** The choice of contrapuntal interval (whether the 3rd, 10th, 6th, 8ve, or unison) must be dictated by the rules of *correct melodic progression.*   For this reason it is necessary to play or sing the added melody, *by itself, after the contrapuntal union has been effected.*   Such a test, applied to Ex. 36, is wholly satisfactory.   Applied to the following ones, it reveals several obvious errors in the added melody, despite the fact that each separate interval is consonant, and that the two melodies, sung or played together, form a harmonious union:

See also Ex. 40, *e.*

45. Furthermore, given the following major melody:

the following counterpoints may be added:

This brief example, simple as it is, should already afford the student a very clear conception of the principle of melody-association, or counterpoint, and an appreciation of its value as a technical exercise. He should compare these three given solutions, and observe how completely the added parts differ from each other; and he may be sure that these are not the only acceptable solutions. Each added part should be played, sung (and conceived mentally, by eye, as usual), first *alone by itself;* then the two melodies must be studied together, and the student must endeavor to conceive their association, mentally, and obtain a perfectly clear impression of their union,— their effect *together.* After doing this very thoroughly,— slowly and thoughtfully,— he must transpose them (by finger and by eye) to G *minor.* And, finally, he must *invert each one of them ;* that is, copy it out, placing the upper part an octave lower, and the lower part an octave higher, than here written.

46. Further, a few inferior and faulty versions, with the same given melody:

Given part.

Explanation. The first half of version *d* is inferior, because the long succession of (parallel) 3rds gives the added part the effect of mere duplication. The same objection partly attends the parallel lines (in 6ths) further on. At the beginning of version *e*, the added part uses the octave three times in succession, which results in exactly similar melodic progressions and defeats the purpose of the union of lines. It is like parallel 3rds and 6ths in principle, but more objectionable. See Rule 2, par. 43.

The rest of version *e* is all poor counterpoint, because of the faulty, awkward leading of the added part, in obvious disregard of the laws of melody. — *Invert both of these versions*, as before.

47. In manipulating a complete sentence, it is desirable that the two parts should not begin with the same beat, in the interest of greater independence. And, as a rule, it is well to end with the octave of the tonic (the keynote in both parts); this, however, is not imperative. For example :

Given melody.

Ex.
41.

or :

Given melody.

EXERCISE 4.

TwO-PART COUNTERPOINT WITH FUNDAMENTAL INTERVALS, MAJOR MODE.

To each of the following given major melodies, a second part is to be added, in corresponding rhythm, according to the above rules, and as shown in Ex. 39.

The given melody is to be used first as upper part, where it is written, and the counterpoint added below. This may be done on the same staff (as in Ex. 39), or upon a separate staff (with bass clef, as seen in Ex. 43, *b* and *c*). The use of two staves is preferable, as it permits greater freedom.

Then the given melody is to be used as lower part, an octave lower than where it is written (or two octaves lower, if necessary), and counterpointed above, — with an added part that differs reasonably from the preceding solution.

Several different versions of the added part should be made in every case, — as was seen in Ex. 39.

12.

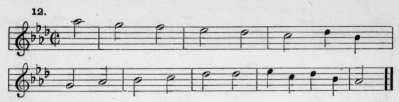

[A solution of Melody 4 will be found in the Appendix, to which the student may refer, after conscientiously completing his own versions.]

Besides these, the student is to write a number of original melodies with added counterpoint, — *designing the melodies together* (as duets). See the Note following Ex. 52.

CHAPTER V.

THE MINOR MODE.

48. As stated in par. 30, all rules of melodic movement in the major mode are valid for minor, with no other modification than that they are applied somewhat more strictly in minor (as far as the movements of the active steps are concerned). Review, carefully, paragraphs 30, 31 and 32, and observe the rule of par. 32,

> that, in minor, the 7th step must be lowered in the descending succession 8-7-6-5 ;
>
> and the 6th step must be raised in the ascending succession 5-6-7-8.

49. Further, all the rules given in Chap. IV for the contrapuntal association of two melodies in major, apply without exception to minor also. The choice of fundamental intervals (3rd, 6th and 8th) for the counterpoint of a given melody is precisely the same in both modes.

It is simply necessary, in minor, to guard the *melodic* progressions more carefully, and to be sure that each part, alone, is a perfectly acceptable melodic line.

50. Given the following minor melody :

Ex. 42.

Its contrapuntal manipulation may result thus :

    a. **Given part, above.**

Ex. 43.

Given part, below.

c. Given part, above.

Explanation. In one instance only, there are four successive 3rds (in version *b*). This should be the limit. The added parts all move with considerable freedom, but are everywhere melodically correct.

At the beginning of measure 3 in version *a*, one note counterpoints two of the given part. In version *c* the added part has a wider range than usual, and diverges farther from the given part (at one point, in the third measure, the two lines are over two octaves apart). This is entirely defensible, as long as the melodies are separately perfect.

Compare the three different added parts, carefully.

EXERCISE 5.

TWO-PART COUNTERPOINT WITH FUNDAMENTAL INTERVALS, MINOR MODE.

Manipulate the following minor melodies, exactly according to the directions given in Exercise 4 : —

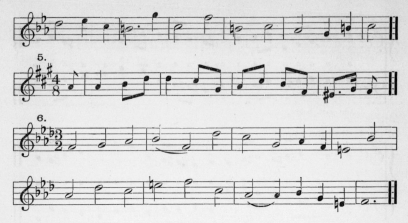

[A solution of Melody 1 will be found in the Appendix.]

Also write, as before, a number of original melodies with counterpoint, *composing the two parts together.* See Note to Ex. 52.

CHAPTER VI.

EXCEPTIONAL INTERVALS.

51. Greater freedom of melodic progression may often be obtained by a few judicious exceptions to the above fundamental rule of harmonious contrapuntal association. While the 3rd, 6th and 8ve are undeniably the most reliable, and must at all times constitute the real basis of the contrapuntal union of parts, there are a few other intervals, mostly of a mildly dissonant character, which, *when used in moderation,* greatly improve the effect, without in the least impairing the general harmonious or consonant character of the sentence as a whole.

52. Rule 4. These secondary intervals, of somewhat exceptional character, are

the **perfect fifth,**

the **augmented fourth,** or **diminished fifth,** and

certain **major seconds,** or **minor sevenths.**

53. The perfect fifth is very rare, and should be used only when it represents the *Dominant* chord (—possibly, more rarely, the Tonic chord).

It can, therefore, occur only singly, — not successively. And it should never appear in inverted form (as perfect fourth). For example:

54. The augmented 4th, and its inversion, the diminished 5th, are fairly common, and always good. In *Major*, they occur only in the chord of the Dom.-7th, as union of steps 4 and 7. For example:

Invert this example; that is, copy it out, placing the upper part an octave lower, and the lower part an octave higher, than here written. *Do this, without fail.*

55. Observe that these intervals are used in counterpointing the tones *b* and *f* in C major,—the 7th and 4th scale-steps.

Observe, further, that the *augmented* interval generally strives "outward," into a larger interval; and that the *diminished* one draws "inward," to a smaller one.

Or, observe simply that the correct resolution of each of these active steps takes care of the melodies.

For further illustration :

The slurs in this example indicate where the *chord remains unchanged,* — a circumstance which always justifies nearly every irregularity. Note this fact well.

Invert this example, as before, and it will illustrate the treatment of the diminished 5th. *Do this, without fail.*

56. In *minor*, the augmented fourth and diminished fifth appear in exactly the same way, at steps 4 and 7, in the chord of the Dom.-7th.

But they also appear (though more rarely) in the union of steps 6 and 2, in minor; possibly also in the union of step 3 and the raised 6th step (par. 32).

As usual, the melodic resolutions must be respected, whereby the results noted in par. 55 will be observed.

Thus (C minor):

57. The minor 7th, and its inversion, the major 2nd, are rare. They should be limited to the union of steps 4 and 5, as part of the chord of the Dom.-7th. Possibly, though very rarely indeed, they may occur as steps 1 and 2, in the II⁷. For illustration (C major and C minor, alike):

Invert this example, as before. Also write it out *in C minor.*

58. Observe that the interval of a 7th draws "inward," and the interval of the 2nd "outward," as a rule. This statement is correct, but not sufficiently explicit. As usual, almost everything depends upon the proper resolution of the active (4th) step. The whole matter may be stated thus:

In the interval of a 7th, the lower tone is a chord-root, the upper tone a chord-seventh. (When inverted, as 2nd, the lower tone is, of course, the chord-seventh.) This tone, — *the chord-seventh*, — generally moves downward one step; but it may remain where it is; and it may make a leap (usually downward) *when the chord remains unchanged.* Thus (C major and C minor):

The slurs again indicate where the chord remains the same, and thus account for the apparent violations of the rule. *Invert this example* for the illustration of the treatment of the interval of a 2nd. *Do this, without fail.* Also write out both versions *in C minor.*

59. For general illustration: Given the following major melody:

Its manipulation may result thus:

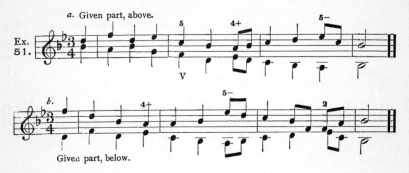

60. Further, in minor:

NOTE. There is not the slightest evidence that either of the two parts, in these two illustrations, was a " given part." Evidently, they were conceived *together*, under the constant influence of the two vital requirements,

(1) perfect melodic formation of each part alone, and

(2) good intervals at the points of contact, to ensure harmonious coöperation.

Invert both of these examples, without fail.

61. Rule 5, — very rare. In minor, it is also possible to use a diminished 7th (and its inversion, an augmented 2nd) in the union of steps 6 and 7 only. They are subject to the usual rules (given in par. 58). Thus:

EXERCISE 6.

FUNDAMENTAL AND SECONDARY INTERVALS; MAJOR AND MINOR MODES.

1. Manipulate Ex. 38 and Ex. 42 again, according to this lesson.
2. Also a few of the given melodies of Exercise 4 and Exercise 5 again.
3. Also the following given melodies, according to former directions, and the rules of this chapter:

[A solution of Melody 5 will be found in the Appendix.]

4. Also write, as usual, a number of original melodies with counterpoint, composing the two parts together, — like Ex. 52.

CHAPTER VII.

RHYTHMIC DIVERSITY. TWO NOTES TO A GIVEN BEAT.

62. The rhythm of the added voice does not always correspond to that of the given melody.   That is, the counterpoint may not only be devised "note against note" in exactly or nearly similar rhythm, as in the preceding lessons, but may run in a more rapid rhythm of two (or more) notes to each note of the given melodic part.

63. When this takes place, — when two or more notes accompany each given note, — a necessary distinction arises, with reference to the relative importance of the several tones in each group (or beat) ; for it is probable that not every single one of the added tones can be of equal harmonic significance.

In making this distinction, the tones are defined as *essential* and *unessential*.   In a group of two notes (against one in the other part), one is usually essential and the other unessential; in a group of three notes, there will generally be one essential and two unessential tones. The distinction is important, because the burden of contrapuntal agreement devolves, naturally, almost wholly upon the essential tones; whereas the unessential ones slip smoothly between, with little or no responsibility.

64. In thus qualifying the tones, the student is influenced largely by the *rhythmic location* of the tones; the one which occupies the accented fraction of the beat is somewhat more likely to be essential, while the un-accented fractions are apt to be filled in with unessential tones. For illustration (the unessential tones marked x):

The *d* and *b* in the first measure are so-called *Passing Notes.*

As may be seen, this counterpoint would be quite perfect if the unes-sential tones (marked x) were all omitted, — thus:

from which the conclusion is drawn, that these tones are unimportant, unessential.

Invert these examples; that is, copy them out, placing the upper part an octave lower, and the lower part an octave higher, than here written.

65. But this is not the only test. The most reliable guide is, after all, the *harmonic quality* of the tone. A tone which is foreign to the chord of the beat cannot be essential; it must be unessential, even when it oc-cupies the accented fraction of its beat. This is seen in Ex. 54; all the tones marked unessential are foreign to the harmony (chord) of the beat, excepting the *d* in the second measure, and the *d* at the end of the third measure. (These two *d*'s are considered unessential, because they are less accented than the harmonic tones which precede them.)

In the following version, with three notes to each one of the given part, some of the unessential tones, foreign to the chord of the beat, ap-pear on the accented fraction:

Ex. 56.

The *f* in the first beat is the " upper Neighbor " of the essential tone *e ;* and the *a* in the second beat of the 3rd measure is the " lower Neighbor " of the essential tone *b.*

Invert this example, as usual. And test it, as before, by omitting all the marked notes; it will agree exactly with Ex. 55.

66. Rule 1. In general, then, all tones that do not constitute a plausible chord-form, that do not belong to the chord which the beat evidently represents, are unessential tones, whether they occupy the unaccented or the accented fraction of the beat. And tones which do form a part of the chord are usually essential. If two or more such chord-tones appear in the same group, only the accented one, however, is regarded as essential; see the first beat in the second measure of Ex. 54 and Ex. 56 (the note *d* in each case).

67. Rule 2. The *essential* tones, in the added part, must be determined precisely as if they stood alone, — note against note, as in former lessons. They are therefore defined according to the table of permissible intervals, 6th, 3rd, 8ve, occasionally the augmented 4th, diminished 5th, and so forth, as has been learned.

This implies that Ex. 54 and Ex. 56 were actually conceived first in the form given in Ex. 55. Such a conclusion is just, to a certain extent; but the unessential tones which " slip smoothly in between " will be found to exert considerable influence upon the counterpoint as a whole, and it is therefore not wise to construct the basis of the contrapuntal part without regard to them. Ex. 55 should not exactly appear as the original, pre-defined form, but rather as the result ; as the form to which Exs. 54 and 56 could be reduced.

68. Rule 3. An *unessential* tone may form *any interval with the given tone,* but its movements are governed strictly by its relation to the essential tone of its group, as follows :

69. Rule 4. In general, an inharmonious interval (that is, a " doubtful " interval, 2nd, 4th, 5th, 7th) should be followed immediately by some " good " interval. Scan Ex. 56 again, with reference to this rule, thus :

Ex. 57.

Explanation. In the first beat, the "poor" interval of a 4th (permitted because the tone is unessential) is immediately followed by the "good" interval of a 3rd. In the second beat, the "poor" 7th (unessential) is followed by the "good" 6th. And so on, throughout.

This being properly provided for, the reduction of the embellished form to the original essential form usually follows as a matter of course. Comp. par. 67.

Invert this example, as usual, and note the change in the interval numbers.

70. Rule 5. Harmonic tones, — such as belong to the chord which the beat represents, — may leap to any other tone of the same chord. This confirms the rule of par. 11. See Ex. 54, the first beat of the second measure ; and the following :

Invert this example, as usual.

71. Rule 6. On the contrary, inharmonic tones, — those not belonging to the chord, — should not leap, but must progress *stepwise. They must be accounted for as passing-notes or neighboring notes which refer diatonically (scalewise) to the following essential tone.* And, as a rule, such tones should not enter with a leap, either. In a word, skips should be limited to harmonic (chord) tones. The following is not good :

To this rule there are two notable exceptions, as follows :

72. Rule 7.

(1) The upper "neighbor" of a chord-tone may leap a 3rd down to the lower neighbor; or the lower neighbor may leap to the upper one ; in other words, the two neighbors of any chord-tone may appear successively, — *if their chord-tone follows,* as resolution of both.

(2) The *upper* "neighbor" may leap down a 3rd, under any circumstances.

The following forms are correct :

Explanation. The tone *f* in the first measure is the upper neighbor of the chord-tone *e* (the I of C major). Instead of moving stepwise, back into *e* (or on up into *g*), it leaps down a 3rd. The irregularity is more fully illustrated in the triplet-figures at *b*.

In measure 2, the tone *b* is the lower neighbor of *c*; it leaps up to *d*, which is the upper neighbor of the same *c*, and then *c* itself appears and resolves them both. In the third measure, *c* and *a* are the two neighbors of the chord-tone *b*, which follows both properly.

It will be observed that the upper neighbor has more liberty than the lower one.

73. Rule 8. Successive octaves (which were proven objectionable in Ex. 34) are not rectified when separated by *one unessential tone,* but may be excused when *an accented essential tone* intervenes (or, possibly, when separated by two unessential tones). Thus:

* * *

74. Reverting to par. 67 (which review), the student may find it help-ful, *at first*, to counterpoint the given melody with essential tones (fundamental intervals) in corresponding rhythm, and then adjust the unessential tones to these (as Ex. 54 was adjusted to Ex. 55).

At all events, such a process is instructive, and worth pursuing for a while.

Given the figure of three ascending scale-steps (upper part of Ex. 62), with a number of possible counterpoints in similar rhythm: —

These simple counterpoints may be transformed into a rhythm of two notes to each beat, as follows :

Compare these two examples carefully (mentally, and also at the keyboard), and observe :

1. That the progressions of the quicker part in Ex. 63 are mostly *stepwise*. Compare par. 71.

2. That when a skip is made, it always represents a good *chord-line*. Compare par. 70.

3. That the unessential tone may lie *between* the beats (unaccented), or may **fall**

upon the beat (accented). See the first and second measures of Ex. 63. Compare par. 65.

4. That two unessential tones may appear in succession, *when the progression is stepwise.* See the first and third measures of Ex. 63.

5. That a rest may sometimes take the place of the *accented* fraction (measure 5). This depends upon what precedes, and is easily controlled. It is common at the very beginning (compare par. 47), but may also occur, occasionally, in the course of the phrase, after a " good " interval.

6. That a direct succession of octaves, or of perfect fifths, is not good; but that the error may be rectified by sufficiently separating the intervals, — see par. 73.

7. That the last three measures of Ex. 63 diverge from the original groups (of Ex. 62). This is because the last unessential tone (the fourth 8th-note), *being a chord-interval,* becomes practically " essential " in character, and therefore chooses its own progression. *This is important, and shows that, ultimately, the student will not first define the essential tones throughout, but will let the choice depend upon momentary conditions, created by the trend of the parts.* Compare, again, par. 67.

75. Quick repetitions should be avoided, as a rule. In their place, the leap of an octave is always permitted, and is extremely effective. Thus, Ex. 64 is awkward; but changed to Ex. 65, the very same notes are excellent:

76. Further, it is by no means necessary that the quicker rhythm should be sustained *in the same part throughout.* For example:

Given part, below.

In measure 3, the given part, itself, has two notes to a beat, and the added part, reversing the rule, relaxes its rhythm and counterpoints one note against two. In the fourth measure (second beat), both parts have the quicker rhythm together.

Such alternation (and occasional union) of rhythmic movement adds greatly to the musical interest of the sentence, without affecting any of the rules.

EXERCISE 7.

TWO-PART COUNTERPOINT, TWO NOTES TO EACH BEAT.

Manipulate the following given melodies, in a constant rhythm of two notes to each beat, — similar to Ex. 66, — using two staves.   Follow the general directions given in Exercise 4.

[A solution of Melody 6 will be found in the Appendix, with which the student may carefully compare his own versions.]

Besides these, re-counterpoint the given melodies of the preceding Exercises, according to the rules of this chapter (with two notes to each beat). The student will do wisely not to neglect this additional task, *for practice is here of the greatest value.*

Also write, as usual, a number of original melodies with counterpoint (as duets) imitating the style of Ex. 66.

CHAPTER VIII.

MODULATIONS.

77. It is neither necessary nor desirable that the added part, or the given melody, should remain in the same key from beginning to end. Modulations in either, or in both, of the parts, are likely to add greatly to the beauty and smoothness of the counterpoint. Such changes of key may be made at any point in the course of a musical sentence, and may be of any reasonable duration, but are subject to certain fairly strict conditions.

78. The most important of these is the limitation naturally imposed by the varying degrees of relation between the keys. Each key is a member of the greater family of keys; each key has its individual place in the system, and stands in perfectly definite relations to the other members of the key family.

79. The proper index of any key in the system of keys is its *Signature;* the number of flats or sharps it contains indicates precisely the degree of similarity or of difference between it and C major, — the central or zero key, the one which has accidentally been chosen for the plain alphabetic letters, without flats or sharps to inflect their pitch. The comparison of the *signatures* therefore exhibits the relative location of the keys, their degrees of similarity or difference, and, consequently, the degrees of *relation* or non-relation. For instance, the two-sharp and three-sharp keys are more nearly related than the two-sharp and the four-sharp, or five-sharp (or any more remote) keys. Also, the two-sharp key is more closely located to the one-sharp, than it is to the zero (the " natural " scale), or any flat key.

80. The *next-related* keys are those whose signatures differ by no more than one similar sign. That is, the two-sharp key is next-related to the one-sharp key (which has only one sharp less); and is also next-related to the three-sharp key (which has only one sharp more). Further, the two-sharp key is next-related, — most closely related, in fact, — to the other key which has the same two-sharp signature; namely, the so-called Relative minor, — or Relative major, as the case may be.

NOTE. This rule of Signature-relations applies, strictly speaking, to major. But it is absolutely valid for both major and minor modes (those with corresponding signatures), because of their very close proximity to each other in the system of keys.

For illustration: D major is next-related to A major, to F-sharp minor, to G major, to E minor, and to B minor.   And B minor (with the same signature) has the same group of next-related keys, — A major, F-sharp minor, G major, E minor, and D major.

Further, the next relatives of a three-flat key are: the two-flat keys, the four-flat keys, and the other key with three flats.   That is, C minor is next-related to B-flat major and G minor, to A-flat major and F minor, and to E-flat major.

N. B. If the student is not *absolutely familiar with all the signatures, major and minor*, he will do well to pause here, and not undertake any exercises in modulation before thoroughly mastering this necessary item of musical knowledge.

81. Rule 1. Modulations that are made during a brief melodic sentence (phrase, period, or double-period) should be limited to the *next-related keys* of the principal or central key.   Thus, a sentence in C major may contain brief modulations into A minor (same signature), into G major or E minor (one-sharp keys), and into F major or D minor (one-flat keys).   A sentence in E-flat major may exhibit transiently the keys of C minor, A-flat major, F minor, B-flat major, or G minor,— any one, or more, or all of these.

For example, a phrase with a three-sharp signature, containing brief excursions into the keys of two and of four sharps (the capital letters indicating major, and the small letters minor):

Ex. 67.

Invert this example, as in the preceding lessons.

82. There are, naturally, other possibilities beyond the closer range of the five next-related keys; such, for instance, as the so-called opposite mode of each related key (that is, the other mode of the *same keynote*,— D major and D minor, etc.).   But in the elementary studies of counterpoint, the next-related keys should suffice for all modulatory changes.

83. Sometimes, as in Ex. 67, the changes of key are indicated by accidentals in the *given* part, in which case they are, of course, obligatory. But it is quite as likely that they may be effected partly, or entirely, in the *added* part, at the option of the student. For example, there are no accidentals in the following given melody, and it may therefore be counterpointed without changes of key, as in the foregoing lessons ; thus (the given part above) :

Invert this example, as usual.

84. Or, this same melody may be counterpointed in such a manner as to contain one or more modulations. For example :

Invert this example, as usual.

85. It is naturally impossible, in these elementary lessons, to give complete explanations and directions for the manifold details of modulation. Besides close attention to the general rules, the student must rely upon his musical judgment to some extent. The main requirements, not only in counterpoint but in music-writing generally, are *smoothness*, and *euphony ;* the union of tones must *sound well*, and each part must *flow easily and naturally*.

Such results can be obtained by every intelligent student who carefully notes the given rules, and who has diligence and patience.

86. Rule 2. The great fundamental rules of modulation are, *to finish one key before passing into another;* and *to enter the new key at some yielding point — not abruptly.*

Technically stated, this means that it is best to close a key (before modulating) upon some form of the Tonic harmony of that key, as this has a concluding quality; and to enter the new key with one of its Dominant (possibly Subdominant) chords, because these lead naturally into the desired Tonic. This may be best illustrated in chord-forms:

Ex. 70.

In every case, here, the keys close upon some form of their Tonic harmony (the I), and each new key begins with some form of its Dominant harmony (the V or V⁷).

Further, in tone-lines:

Ex. 71.

Invert this example, as usual.

Observe, that both here and in Ex. 70 only the keys of one flat and one sharp are represented, as nearest relatives of the principal key (C major, zero signature). Observe, also, that each key terminates with a Tonic impression, and that each modulation is made through the Dominant harmony of the desired key; in one case only (at the end) the new key begins with a Subdominant harmony (the II).

Also analyze Ex. 67, with reference to the chords employed in modulating.

87. In the following example (Ex. 72) most of the changes of key are made by means of a *chromatic* movement.

88. Rule 3. When a modulation is made chromatically, it is generally needless to regard the fundamental rule (par. 86); that is, when the chromatic inflection is used, it does not matter at what harmonic point the old key is abandoned. But the new key *is generally entered through its dominant or subdominant,* in any case. For illustration:

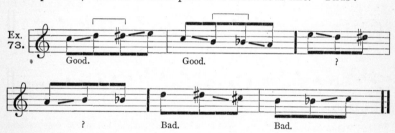

Invert this example, as usual. And analyze it carefully, with reference to the key-relations and the chords. Also analyze Ex. 69.

89. It is evident, then, that modulations may be made most freely and easily by means of the chromatic change. On the other hand, the manner of treating *the chromatic change itself* is subject to stricter regulations. Namely:

90. Rule 4. Chromatic changes are usually good; but they should not be made too rapidly (as a general rule not quicker than eighth-notes); and *the chromatic movement should be introduced in the corresponding direction* if possible, — so as to form part of a continuous line. Thus:

Examine Ex. 72 again, and observe the straight-forward manner in which each chromatic progression is introduced, and how it continues in the same direction. There is one exception, — at the end of the third measure (in the lower part); the upward chromatic move is preceded by a leap, downward, and therefore confirms the rule of "turning after a wide leap" (par. 16). The same thing occurs at the beginning of Ex. 71, in the lower part.

EXERCISE 8.

TWO-PART COUNTERPOINT, WITH CHANGES OF KEY.

1. Manipulate the following melodies, *in corresponding rhythm* (as in Exercises 4, 5 and 6, and examples 71 and 72), modulating wherever possible or necessary. In the first three melodies, the * indicates where changes of key are to be made. Use each melody twice, first as upper and then as lower part, as usual:

1.

2, Manipulate the following melodies in a constant rhythm of *two notes to each beat* (as in Exercise 7) *with modulations,* similar to Ex. 67 and Ex. 69. Use two staves, as a rule.

(6 notes.)

[A solution of Melody 11 will be found in the Appendix.]

3. Also experiment with some melodies of the preceding Exercises, with a view to possible modulations in the *added part*,— on the principle of examples 68 and 69 (review pars. 83 and 84).

4. Also write, as usual, a number of original melodies with counterpoint.

CHAPTER IX.

THREE NOTES TO A BEAT.

91. When the rhythm of the added part is again quickened, so that *three* tones accompany each beat of the given part, there will generally be one essential tone, and two unessential ones, in each group.

92. The rules governing these are exactly the same as before (Chap. VII):

1. The essential tones are chosen according to the fundamental rule of good intervals (6th, 3rd, 8ve; occasionally the perfect 5th, diminished 5th, augmented 4th, etc.).

2. The unessential tones may form any interval.

3. The quicker part *runs chiefly stepwise* (smoothly); but may leap, along any good chord-line.

4. Successive 8ves and perfect 5ths should be avoided.

5. Each part must be melodically perfect, in and by itself.

6. The essential tone generally stands at the beginning of the group (on the accented fraction), — but by no means necessarily.

7. Either "neighbor" of a harmonic tone may leap (a 3rd) to the other neighbor, on condition that the principal (harmonic) tone *follows*, and resolves both. Par. 72, (1).

8. The *upper* "neighbor" may occasionally leap down a 3rd, without this condition (usually in the *upper* part). Par. 72, (2).

For illustration :

Also, with greater freedom :

93. Further, with occasional irregular movements :

In group 1, the two neighbors, *b* and *d*, precede their principal tone *c* (par. 92–7). Exactly the same thing takes place in groups 2 and 3 ; but observe the change in their location in the group. In group 5, the upper neighbors leap down a 3rd, without ultimate resolution (par. 92–8; see also Ex. 60, *b*).

In inverting these examples, the student will learn that the result is perfectly good in every instance, — excepting Ex. 75, group 5. That is, all these irregularities are permissible in either the upper or the lower part, — excepting that of par. 92–8, which, if used, should be carefully tested.

94. Further, with alternating rhythmic movement (review par. 76) :

Ex. 76.

Invert this example, as usual.

In the first beat of the third measure, the 7th scale-step (*g-sharp*) is lowered to *g-natural*, because it descends. In the first beat of the last measure the 6th scale-step (*f*) is raised to *f-sharp*, because it ascends. Compare par. 32, and Ex. 30.

95. As the rhythm quickens and the tones multiply, in this manner, the principle of par. 28 becomes more and more imperative.

Review par. 28 thoroughly, and endeavor to apply *the rule of the sequence, and of uniform grouping generally*, as much as possible in the running part.

For example: The following two versions are both faultless counterpoint; but version *b* is far better music than version *a* because the uniform arrangement of its groups gives it a more definite character, and clearer significance than the other,—which creates a more rambling, purposeless impression.

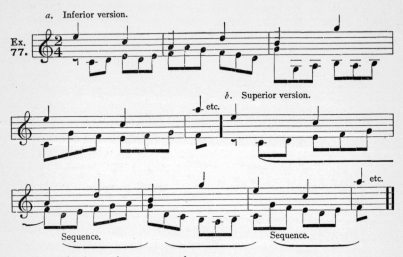

Invert both versions, as usual.

EXERCISE 9

Three Notes to a Beat.

Manipulate the following melodies (each one twice, as usual), in a constant rhythm of three notes to each beat (as triplets). Use two staves, as a rule:

[A solution of Melody 4 will be found in the Appendix.]

Besides these, manipulate some of the given melodies of the preceding Exercises.

And, as usual, write a number of original melodies with counterpoint, imitating the style of the above.

CHAPTER X.

SYNCOPATION, OR SHIFTED RHYTHM.

96. Another method of obtaining quicker rhythm in the counterpoint of a given melody, consists in simply *shifting the tones of the added part forward,* so that they fall between (instead of upon) the beats. The re-

sult is syncopation, and is invariably permissible when applied to a counterpoint that is *entirely smooth and faultless* to begin with.   (Comp. par.
108.)

97.   For illustration: The following faultless series of intervals, in
corresponding rhythm:

will produce the effect of quickened rhythm (two notes to each beat),
when the lower part is thus *shifted forward:*

or when the lower part remains, and the upper part is *shifted forward:*

98.   This process involves the *Tie,* — a device which the student must
regard as one of the most important and effective means of relieving the
monotony of the rhythm and of increasing the energy of the musical sentence.

When obtained in the above manner, as modification of a perfectly
good interval-succession, the tie is as reliable as it is valuable, and suggests no other objection than that of possible monotony.

99. But this possible monotony may be easily avoided, either by using the tie in alternating parts, or by employing it occasionally only, instead of constantly.

In the following examples the parts are *alternately* syncopated (in two of an almost endless variety of forms):

And in the following, the tie is used *occasionally*, alternating with passing-notes as defined in a preceding lesson:

100. The same principle applies, naturally, to an original counter-point of *two* notes to each beat, which, — if smooth and faultless in itself, — may be accelerated to a rhythm of three notes to each beat, by means of the tie and shifted rhythm. Thus, the following faultless counterpoint:

Ex. 83.

may be quickened to this:

101. The greatest emphasis must be laid upon the necessity of avoiding all doubtful or irregular conditions, in the original construction of the counterpoint that is to be manipulated in these syncopated forms. Only the smoothest and most perfect models can be thus utilized.

EXERCISE 10.

SHIFTED RHYTHM AND TIES; TWO AND THREE NOTES TO A BEAT.

Manipulate the following melodies, according to the above rules, as follows:

1. Construct (with each given melody) a faultless counterpoint in corresponding rhythm (like Ex. 78), and alter this to various accelerated forms with two notes to each ·beat (as in Exs. 79 to 82). At least six different versions of each melody should be obtained. Each melody to be used both as upper and as lower part, as usual.

2. Construct a faultless counterpoint with two notes to each beat (as in Exercise 7), and modify this to various accelerated forms with three notes to each beat (as in Ex. 83).

3. Besides these, experiment with some of the counterpoints constructed in earlier exercises (possibly omitting Exercise 6, because of the irregularities), modifying them to quicker rhythms. *This may be done at sight, at the keyboard.*

CHAPTER XI.

THE TIE, CONTINUED. RESTS.

102. It is also possible, of course, to introduce a tie without such reference to a pre-defined counterpoint as formed the basis of the preceding lesson. But in this case, — if the student undertakes to make independent use of the tie, — it is necessary that the nature of this technical device should be more fully understood.

103. Ties differ greatly in their effect. The longer tone, which results from using a tie, and therefore consists of portions of two contiguous beats (or measures), may produce a gentle strain upon the second beat ; or, on the contrary, it may prove to be a dead weight upon both beats. Compare the two different applications of the tie in the following :

NOTE. In order to distinguish easily and quickly, we shall call the first of the two tied notes the "tying" note; and the second one the "tied" note. In the first group, the *d* at the end of the first measure is the *tying* note, the next *d* (at the beginning of the second measure) is the *tied* note.

In the first group (Ex. 84), the tied note appears to vitalize the rhythm and melody, because it is a foreign tone and strives for resolution. Such tones are called Suspensions, because they hold the correct harmonic tone "in suspense." Here, the second *d* "suspends" the real chord-tone *c*.

In the second group the tie acts as an incubus upon both melody and rhythm. The tying note (the first *c*) is called an Anticipation, because it does not belong to the chord of its beat, but "anticipates" the harmonic tone of the next beat. While such tones are sometimes used with striking effect, they are, *when tied*, usually disappointing.

104. A similar paralyzing effect is generally created when the tied note is longer than the tying note. And, in any case, it is not wise to leave the tying note very short; it (the note where the tie begins) should not, as a rule, be less than a half-beat.

For example:

The second group is not wholly wrong, as the tied note is a suspension; and suspensions are rarely limited in their time-value. Groups 1 and 4 are intolerable, because the tying notes are abrupt anticipations.

NOTE. *When the tones are struck, instead of being tied, the case is entirely different;* omitting the ties, the above are all possible. *But see par. 75,* and note the analogy between that rule and this one.

105. Rule 1. In using a tie, it is always best to make the tied note (the second one of the two) a suspension. In other words, *the tied tone had best be foreign to the harmony of its beat,* and then progress stepwise into the essential harmonic tone. In still other words, it is usually best to tie *from one of the "good" intervals* (3rd, 6th, 8th, augmented 4th, etc.) *over into a "poor" one.* Thus:

In the first measure, an 8th (good interval) is tied over into a 7th (poor interval); then a 6th is tied over into a 5th, — and so on.

In the last measure, the suspension *f* is treated as upper neighbor, and carried over into the lower neighbor before resolving to *e*. See par. 92–7.

The whole example may, it is true, be reduced to a series of good essential intervals, from which it may appear to have been derived. This goes to prove that the simple process of *syncopation* explained in the preceding lesson (Exs. 78 to 82) is likely to prove quite sufficient for the ordinary applications of the tie, though it covers a narrower range of possibilities.

Invert Ex. 86, as usual, copying it out, and placing the upper part an octave lower, and the lower part an octave higher, than here written.

106. In the above example, each tied note was a suspension; the effect is therefore good.

When, on the contrary, the rule is reversed, and the tying note is an anticipation, the result is as follows:

Ex. 87.

107. Here, poor intervals are tied over into good ones. The effect is decidedly inferior to that of Ex. 86, and would be intolerable but for the significant fact that this condition prevails *throughout ;* the device of anticipation is applied *persistently and uniformly.* Such consistency is an excuse for almost any irregularity.

108. This example, if reduced to its essential intervals, will be found to differ vitally from those of the preceding chapter. There, one of the parts was shifted forward; *here, one of the parts is shifted backward.* Evidently, both methods are possible; but it is surely far better to shift one part **forward** (par. 96).

109. Rule 2. It is also permissible to tie one good interval over into another good one; that is, to use the tie for a tone that is common to both beats. In this case, skips may occur, of course. For example:

Ex. 88.

Invert this example, as usual.

This arrangement of the intervals occurs quite frequently in Exs. 79 to 82,— which should now be analyzed with reference to these more general rules of **the tie.**

There, not every tied note is a suspension, but often a " good " interval,—in exact keeping with the faultless model, from which it was derived by merely shifting the notes forward.

110. Another important device for increasing the effectiveness of a tone-line, especially in counterpoint, is the *short Rest.*

111. Rule 3. It is a somewhat singular fact that a rest (uniform in value with the general rhythm of the part) may always be substituted for the tied note (on the accented fraction). Thereby the tie simply drops out, but its effect is retained. For illustration, Ex. 86 may be written as follows :

Ex. 89.

Invert these as usual.

The third version of the above example contains too many rests ; the melody loses its cohesion and force. The fourth version is also inferior, because the rests are irregularly distributed ; the melody loses its evenness of structure, and becomes spasmodic.

112. From this it appears that *occasional* brief rests, on *corresponding beats,* yield the best results. The student may experiment (at the keyboard) with Exs. 87 and 88; also with Exs. 79 to 83, — introducing rests.

113. Rule 4. A tied note may be followed : —

1. By its proper *stepwise resolution*, if it is an inharmonic suspension (as in Ex. 86): or by any good leap, if it chances to be an harmonic interval (as in Ex. 88).

2. By the *other neighbor* of the resolving tone, — leaping a 3rd, up or down as the case may be, as in Ex. 86, last measure (and Ex. 90, *a*).

3. By a *repetition of the tied note* (Ex. 90, *b*).

114. The first of these methods is, of course, always good and always applicable. The second and third are peculiarly useful in quicker rhythms (of 3 or 4 notes to a beat). For illustration, Ex. 86 may be accelerated from two notes to three in each beat, in the following ways :

a. (Double-neighbors.)

b. (Repetitions.)

c. (Rests.)

d. (Alternating rhythms, par. 99.)   *The best form.*

(*a* and *b* mixed.)

etc.

Invert each of these examples as usual.

Observe that these methods, Rule 4, apply best to the note which is legitimately tied as a result of shifting the original essential interval *forward;* not so well to the tie which creates an anticipation (Ex. 87).

EXERCISE II.

Ties and Rests; Two and Three Notes to a Beat.

1. Add a contrapuntal part to each of the following melodies, in a rhythm of **two** notes to each beat, *with ties,* as in Ex. 86.

The tie need not be used in every group; the occasional omission of the tie, and substitution of passing-notes, is not only effective, but often convenient. See par. 99 (Ex. 82).

Each melody to be used as upper, and also as lower part, as usual.

N. B. The student must remember that in case of embarrassment, it is always permissible to fall back upon the process given in pars. 96, 97.

5.

2. Each version thus obtained is then to be quickened into a rhythm of *three* notes to each beat, according to the above rules (pars. 111, 113, — Ex. 90). At least four different forms of each should be written out; and still other versions may be made at sight, at the keyboard.

[A solution of Melody 3 will be found in the Appendix.]

3. Besides these, write a number of original melodies with counterpoint, as usual, composing the parts *together*.

CHAPTER XII.

FOUR NOTES TO A BEAT.

115. When four notes accompany one beat-note of the given part, there will be one essential tone and three unessential ones, or two essential and two unessential ones, in each group. All the rules given in the preceding chapters are valid, without exception or modification, for these still quicker rhythmic movements ; but the larger the groups, the greater the likelihood and necessity of uniform figures, and of more definite formations, in general.

116. Among many forms which four-tone groups are apt to assume, the following figures are especially common and worthy of notice :

Ex.
91.

In group 1, the upper neighboring note (*f*) is so inserted as to create a 3-tone figure out of the essential tone (*e*) ; the final unessential tone (*d*) goes on to *c*, or back to *e*, as the next beat may require. In group 2, the lower neighbor is used in the same way. In groups 3 and 4, the double-neighbor is so used as to transform the essential tone at once into a four-tone figure.

117. Applied to a faultless series of good essential intervals :

The results may be, — using only the above figures :

Invert all of these, as usual.

At N.B., in the second measure of version *a*, the lower neighbor is *g-sharp* instead of *g*. In many cases, this choice of the *half-step for the lower neighbor* is decidedly preferable. It is left to the taste of the student, who therefore should not neglect to test the lower neighbor, and substitute the half-step (with an accidental) where it sounds better.

The *upper* neighbor always agrees with the scale.

118. Rule 1. The direction of the figure, when a double-neighbor is used, — of which the two possibilities are indicated in version *b* of the above example, — depends mainly upon the location of the following essential tones, which should, as a rule, be approached in a straight line. For example :

119. Rule 2. It is usually unwise to leap to the first (accented) tone of a following beat, *after stepwise progression in the same direction* up to that point. This is important. In other words, do not interrupt a stepwise progression (in the *same* direction) at the junction of one group with the next; if a skip is necessary, make it earlier in the group. For illustration:

The ear follows up a stepwise progression, and if it extends to the end of its group, the ear (mental ear) expects that it will *continue stepwise into the next beat.* Compare groups 1 and 3, for an illustration of this cause of mental disappointment.

Group 4 is wrong in any case, because of the rule in par. 71 (Ex. 59), which see.

In group 6, the *c-sharp* is preferable to *c*, because the essential intervals impart an impression of *D* minor. Further, the *c* is possibly the unessential lower neighbor of *d*, and therefore sounds best as half-step, — compare note to Ex. 93 (N. B.).

Observe that, in groups 3 and 7, there *is* a leap into the new group, but it is not in the same direction as the stepwise tones that precede it.   Such a change of direction is generally good.   Group 8 is very peculiar; but correct, because of the distinctly unessential nature of the notes that cause the irregularities. Analyze thoughtfully, and test at the piano.

120.   Other manipulations of Ex. 92 :

Study these carefully.   Invert them all, as usual.

In version 1, second measure, there is a wide leap at the junction of the groups. It is daring, because it is a skip to an inharmonic tone. See, again, par. 71 (Ex. 59). It is permissible, however, because (like Ex. 95, No. 8) the nature of the unessential tones is so entirely unmistakable ; and, further, because of the analogy between the groups in that measure and the next (each group beginning with a " neighbor,"— compare par. 107, last sentence).

Observe that in all of these versions, and in nearly all recent examples, one of the parts usually carries on the quicker rhythm for a beat or so, at the cadence.

121. Rule 3. It is permissible, and desirable, to use *successive chord-tones occasionally.* Thus:

Ex. 97.

Invert, as usual.

This style, however, suggests " harmonic " figuration rather than "melodic " progression, and should therefore be used sparingly. Preference should be given to stepwise progressions, especially to such straight lines (fairly long) as are seen in many places in Ex. 96.

122. Rule 4. Besides the " straight lines " just mentioned, the most desirable and necessary trait in counterpoint is the *sequence, and uniformity of figures in general.* Review, carefully, par. 95 (Ex. 77, *b*) ; and reflect that this requirement is more imperative in counterpoint with four notes to a beat, than in the preceding, less active, varieties. For further illustration :

Ex. 98.

G major.

Invert this, as usual.

EXERCISE 12.

Two-Part Counterpoint. Four Notes to Each Beat.

Add a contrapuntal part to each of the following given melodies, in a rhythm of four notes to each beat, — without ties. Each melody is to be used both as upper and as lower part, as usual; and several different versions of each should be obtained. Use two staves, as a rule.

[A solution of Melody 2 will be found in the Appendix.]

Besides these, re-counterpoint some of the melodies given in Exercises 4, 5, 6 and 7, according to this chapter.

Also write, as usual, a number of original melodies with counterpoint.

CHAPTER XIII.

FOUR NOTES TO A BEAT, AS AMPLIFIED FORMS.

123. The principle of paragraphs 96 and 100 (which review) is applicable also to the contrapuntal rhythm of four tones to a beat. Namely: An original counterpoint of *three* notes to each beat, if smooth and faultless, may be accelerated to a rhythm of four notes, by means of the tie and shifted rhythm.

For example:

124. It will be observed that these results are not as good as those of the former chapter (pars. 96 and 100). The chief drawback is the *brevity of the tying-note,* which, in this quicker movement, is only a quarter of a beat. See par. 104, second sentence. Another drawback is the circumstance that the tied note is frequently a " good " interval instead of an inharmonic one. See par. 105.

The excuse for both of these unfavorable conditions is their *persistency* (par. 107, last sentences), but even that is a source of monotony. They are improved by inserting an occasional brief rest, as shown in Ex. 106.

Therefore, the student will probably not make extensive use of this device, *in this quicker grade of movement,* but depend upon other, better resources, as follows :

125. A counterpoint of four notes to a beat may also be derived from a faultless version of *two* notes to each beat, by embellishing the first note of each two-tone group with its upper or lower neighbor, — as already shown in Ex. 91.

The *upper* neighbor is generally chosen when the two-note group is a *falling figure;* and the *lower* neighbor, when it is a *rising figure.* Thus :

At *a,* the figure ascends; therefore it is better to use the lower neighbor (*b*) of the first note (*c*). At *b,* the opposite applies.

126. For illustration, the following faultless counterpoint of " two against one " :

becomes amplified to four-tone groups, by such embellishment of each accented fraction :

Invert these examples, as usual.

127. Further, a perfect counterpoint of "two against one" may be accelerated to four-tone groups by inserting a *chord-tone* (instead of the upper or lower neighbor) between the first tone (of each group) and its repetition.

Observe the manner in which such a "repetition" always occurs when a tone is embellished by its neighbor, — as in Exs. 91 and 100. That is, the principal tone always recurs, after the neighboring note.

Thus, when applied to Ex. 101 :

Invert this example.

In order to apply this last device correctly, the student must be able to **define** the chords. This should not be difficult, for in all good counterpoint the chord-succession is a ruling factor, and at least always present to a recognizable degree.

128. Further, two tones may become *three, or four*, by applying the octave-leap (par. 75) to the first tone of each group. Thus, with reference to Ex. 101 :

This form, though perfectly legitimate, is best limited to *occasional* use; its constant employment yields somewhat awkward results.

129. The best products are obtained, as usual, by employing all of these forms of enlargement, as shown in Exs. 91, 99, 102, 103 and 104, in rational alternation. For instance:

Ex. 105.

130. The brief rest may be used in connection with the tie, as shown in Ex. 89. (Review par. 111 and par. 112.)

Applied to Ex. 99, *c*, the result might be:

Ex. 106.

This version is considerably better than Ex. 99, *c*.

131. These various methods of obtaining a more animated contrapuntal part by simply expanding the simple small groups, or even the single essential tones, are as significant as they are natural and convenient; because, as the student has no doubt already observed, the most elaborate contrapuntal results are invariably reducible to a simple basis, and are, naturally, nothing more than an amplification of the latter.

All composition is, technically speaking, the development of the resources contained within the primary chord or chords, by familiar devices of rhythm, figuration, duplication, and the like. The most brilliant florid passages in the works of Liszt, Chopin, and other pianoforte writers, can always be reduced to the three or four tones of which the chord is composed, — multiplied, usually, by the addition of the grace-notes (inharmonic neighboring notes) which occupy the spaces between and around the chord-tones themselves. The most hasty analysis of any apparently elaborate piano composition will convince the student of this fact, and lead him to realize the extreme importance and correctness of all the processes of amplification, — of the development of larger groups of tone out of the simplest smaller groups.

EXERCISE 13.

Four Notes to Each Beat.

1. Add a contrapuntal part to each of the following melodies, in a rhythm of *two notes* to each beat.   Then accelerate each version to a rhythm of *four tones* to each beat, by the means shown in paragraphs 125, 127, 128 ; particularly par. 129.   Each melody to be manipulated both as upper and as lower part.   Two staves will generally be necessary.

2. Add a contrapuntal part to each, in a rhythm of *three notes* to each beat, and quicken to a rhythm of four notes by means of the tie (and occasional rest) as shown in Exs. 99 and 106.

3. Manipulate some of the two-note counterpoints of Exercise 7 and Exercise 8, section 2 ; and the three-note counterpoints of Exercise 9 ; accelerating them to four-tone groups according to this chapter.   Some of this expansion may be done at sight, at the keyboard.

CHAPTER XIV.

DIVERSITY OF RHYTHMIC MOVEMENT.

132. If the student who has conscientiously worked out the foregoing exercises in two-part counterpoint has at last become somewhat oppressed with their monotonous character, and has grown tired of them, it is no reflection upon his own good taste, or upon the technical correctness of this particular species of tone association.   The defect lies in the *absence of rhythmic interest,* which must necessarily attend exercises of this **kind,**

with their humdrum pace of two, three, or four uniform notes to each uniform beat, in one of the two melody-parts. So important is the element of rhythm, so indispensable is a certain amount of rhythmic diversity, that no musical sentence is complete and effective without it. A contrapuntal phrase may be perfect in every harmonic and melodic respect, and yet fail to excite interest or real enjoyment, because of a lack of rhythmic variety.

Consequently, no union of contrapuntal parts may be called wholly acceptable, if it does not exhibit more or less diversity of time-values in either, or both, of the parts; it must bear witness to a life within, pulsing with the varying stress of human emotion.

133. To some extent, this important requirement has already been taken into consideration, in the preceding lessons. Review par. 76 and 94, — Examples 66 and 76. It is possible, however, to develop and systematize the process of diversifying the general rhythmic effect of a musical sentence, and to define the method of its application.

134. In order to fix the bounds of such rhythmic diversity, and prevent any extravagance of rhythmic effect, it is customary to preserve a *general uniformity of time-value* (a certain constant fundamental movement), and to limit the diversity of rhythm to the *alternating* interaction of the parts. That is, instead of giving all the more rapid tones to either one of the contrapuntal parts alone (as in most of the preceding exercises), they should be distributed alternately between the parts, — not in such regular intervals as to incur again monotony of another kind, but so as to impart a more definite melodic character to each separate part, without disturbing the evenness of the whole.

135. For illustration, an example like the following, with *constant uniform rhythm* in the added part, —

may be made far more vital and significant in *both* parts, by some such alternation of the fundamental movement (three notes to each beat) as this :

In both of these diversified versions it will be observed that the original intervals, marked in Ex. 107, are retained without essential change. At *a* (Ex. 108), the rapid tones are assigned first to one, and then to the other, of the two parts, in regular alternation, — from measure to measure. At *b* the effect is still further improved by a more irregular distribution of the shorter tones. First of all, it will be seen that they are not confined to one part at a time, but appear occasionally in *both parts at once* (on the second beat of the first and second measures) ; further, the movement in general is more animated than at *a*, — the upper part quickens at every second beat, and the lower part has nearly constant rapid rhythm; interrupted just often enough to prevent monotony. A clear impression of the increased melodic vitality and beauty of these versions can be best obtained by singing each part alone. Do this thoughtfully, first with the separate parts of Ex. 107, and then with those of Ex. 108. Also invert both examples, as usual, copying them out and placing the upper part an octave lower, and the lower part an octave higher, than here written.

136. Further, in a rhythm of four notes to each original beat (on the basis of the essential intervals given in Ex. 107):

Examine these two versions carefully, and invert them, as usual. Sing each part alone.

137. Rule 1. The effect of *uniform rhythmic movement* should be preserved. That is, the general rhythm (two, three, or four notes to a beat, as the case may be) should be maintained in one part or the other, — occasionally in both together, as seen in the above examples.

Rare exceptions to this rule may be made, at *accented* points (as shown in the next example).

In Ex. 108 there is no beat which has less or more than the adopted rhythm of three tones ; and in Ex. 109 every beat has its four tones, in one or the other of the parts.

138. An occasional interruption (slackening) of the fundamental movement is shown in the following, — applied correctly at *a*, incorrectly at *b* :

The stars indicate where the steady running movement is interrupted. In version *a* these interruptions all occur at accented points (at the beginning of each measure); therefore they are all correct. In version *b* they all occur at comparatively unaccented points, and are therefore irregular. Review, carefully, par. 22 and par. 23. Hence :

139. Rule 2. In case of any diversity of time-values in the collective rhythmic formation of a sentence, *the heavier (longer) tones should generally occur at accented points.*

The demonstration is obvious : — Longer notes are " heavier " notes, and belong properly to the comparatively " heavy " points in the measure (or beat) ; shorter notes are " lighter," and belong properly to the comparatively " light " points.

Examine Ex. 110 very minutely with reference to this distinction.

140. It must be distinctly understood that this rule does not apply, necessarily, to each separate part, but to the *combined effect of both together* (that is, to the collective rhythmic formation). If either one of the two parts maintains the fundamental movement, the result will probably be good.

At the same time, it is usually necessary to avoid any striking irregularities *in the upper part*, because that is the more prominent one. For instance, the following version is not quite as smooth as Ex. 110, *a :*

In Ex. 110, *a*, the lighter tones (16th-notes) in the upper part all appear on the lighter beat (second, or unaccented beat) of each measure. Here, in Ex. 111, on the contrary, the heavy (first) beat is subdivided into the light 16th-notes, while the unbroken (heavy) quarter-notes fall on the unaccented beats. Sing each of these two upper parts *alone*, and note the marked difference in their effect. Observe, also, that Ex. 111, *when inverted*, sounds perfectly well.

141. This warning applies chiefly to the quicker rhythmic movements. It is seldom necessary in rhythms of only two notes to a beat; but becomes so in a rhythm of three, and is still more imperative in one of four notes to a beat.

In *slower* rhythmic movement, and moderate tempo, even the fundamental rule (par. 139) may often be disregarded. For example :

Here, the comparatively heavier notes all stand upon the lighter beats of the measure; but the effect is not bad. Observe that in measures 2, 3 and 4 they occur *uniformly* on the second beat. See par. 23, second sentence (Ex. 23). Invert this example.

EXERCISE 14.

Rhythmic Movement in Alternating Parts.

Add a contrapuntal part to each of the following melodies, in *corresponding rhythm* (note against note, as in Exercise 4), being careful to select good essential intervals, as required in par. 101, — which review.

Each version thus obtained is then to be amplified into a rhythm of first two, then three, and then four notes to each beat, — the rhythmic movement to appear alternately (and occasionally together) in the two parts, as shown in the above examples. Use two staves, as a rule.

Par. 95.

Par. 190.

Par. 192.

Besides these, experiment with some former melodies.

Also invent a number of *original melodies with counterpoint*, as usual, imitating the style of the above, in sentences of four, six, or eight measures.

CHAPTER XV.

MOTIVE-DEVELOPMENT. IMITATION.

142. The student may now venture to make more specific practical application of the contrapuntal facility he has gained ; for the beginner, this is most easily and safely effected in the manipulation and development of a brief *Motive.*

143. The general aim of counterpoint, as stated, is the association of melodies, or the multiplication of melodic lines by harmonious coöperation. But the mere increase of the number of melodic parts is, in itself, no guaranty of artistic structure ; on the contrary, such profusion of lines may easily tend to render the structure complex and obscure, and defeat the artistic purpose by diffusion instead of concentration. Multiplicity of tone-lines may so divide the hearer's attention as to destroy his sense of the principal line or lines of the musical picture.

The necessary concentration is gained *by the adoption of some striking motive, or leading figure,* which is held more or less constantly before the hearer's mind, as the ruling idea, in the development of which all the parts engage alternately.

Very many devices are employed in this process of development ; for the explanation of these, the student is referred to the author's "Applied Counterpoint," Chap. IV ; or any standard text-book. Only the most natural and fundamental method can be considered here.

144. A Motive is a brief melodic sentence, usually no more than one or two measures in length ; of simple, regular, but somewhat striking character.   It may begin at any point in the measure, and with any tone which indicates or suggests the tonic chord of the key ; it generally ends upon an accented beat, with some tone of the tonic (or, more rarely, the dominant) chord.   It is chiefly necessary to provide for a clear *tonic* impression, at, or near, the beginning, so as to establish the key, and obviate any awkward or obscure conditions further on.

For illustrations of Motive construction, the student is referred to the Two-part and Three-part Inventions of **Bach,** almost all of which begin with the "Motive" (contained in the first measure or two).   Sometimes the motive appears alone, as in Nos. 1, 2, 3 and 4 of the Two-part Inventions.   Sometimes it is accompanied at once by a *lower* contrapuntal part, as in Nos. 1, 2, 3 and 4 of the Three-part Inventions. *Examine all of these motives very carefully ;* and also the following two, which will be employed in this lesson :

1. G major.   Motive.

Ex.
113.

2. D minor. Motive.

145. The first and most natural act in the development of a Motive, is its recurrence, — not in the same part, *but in the other part.* Such a reproduction of the Motive in another part is called its *Imitation* (not " repetition "). See Ex. 114, second measure. The term Imitation may be applied to each successive occurrence of the Motive, throughout the sentence; though the proper name " Motive " is everywhere quite sufficient.

146. The design of a sentence that is devoted to the manipulation of a Motive, in two-part counterpoint, is as follows:

1. The adopted Motive is first announced, generally alone, in either the upper or lower of the two parts of which the contrapuntal sentence is to consist. Then it is taken up, — or " imitated," — by the other part; usually upon the same beats of the measure as at first; and upon the same steps of the scale, either an octave higher, or an octave lower, than before (according to the location of the leading part).

2. A recurrence of that kind, upon the same steps of the higher or lower octave, is called the " Imitation in the octave." See Ex. 114, second measure, upper part.

3. Meanwhile, *the first part continues its melodic movement,* as contrapuntal " added part " to the Motive which is being imitated in the other part. This continuation is called the " Contrapuntal associate."

4. This counterpoint is made according to the principles and rules of the preceding chapters, particularly chapter XIV, with reference to the free rhythmic treatment of the two parts.

5. But it is subject to one other significant rule; namely: The contrapuntal associate must be a *perfectly natural continuation of the preceding tones,* so adjusted and conducted that the entire group appears to be one uninterrupted melodic sentence.

147. These details are all exhibited in the following examples (with the Motives of Ex. 113):

Ex.
114.

Motive.

G major.

Imitation (in the 8ve.).

Contrapuntal associate.

This is analyzed as follows: First, the "announcement" of Motive 1 (Ex. 113) in the lower part; followed by its "Imitation" an octave higher, in the upper part; and, below, the "contrapuntal associate" of this Imitation of the Motive.

Play, or sing, the lower part alone, in order to test the above rule (146–5), and prove that these two measures (in the lower part) are an entirely complete and satisfactory melodic phrase, by themselves, without regard to the Motive in the other part.

Further (with Motive 2 of Ex. 113):

Ex.
115.

Motive.
D minor.

Contrapuntal associate.

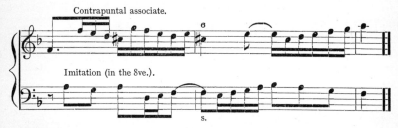

Imitation (in the 8ve.).

s.

Here the Motive is announced in the upper part, and imitated an octave below in the lower part. Again, play or sing the upper part alone, throughout, and test these two measures with reference to the rule in par. 146–5.

148. In order to obtain a better grasp of these important preliminary details, the student may re-write these two examples, reversing the order of the parts. Namely: Begin Ex. 114 with the Motive in the upper part; imitate it in the lower (in the octave), but invent a *new* contrapuntal associate, adopting a different melodic and rhythmic form from the one given above.

Then begin Ex. 115 with the Motive in the lower part, imitation in the upper, and new contrapuntal associate.

Also examine the first few measures of the Two-part Inventions of **Bach,** Nos.
1, 2, 3, 4, 7, and 8; observe the manner of imitation (in every case in the lower part),
and carefully analyze the formation of the contrapuntal associate.

In No. 10 of these Inventions, the imitation of the motive (second measure,
lower part), is not in the octave, but a *fourth* below the original tones. From this it
will be inferred that the motive may recur upon any steps of the scale which may
prove to be convenient for the purpose. The imitation in the octave (upon the same
steps) is, however, by far the most common *at the beginning;* while other steps of
the scale are likely to be chosen for the reappearances of the motive from time to
time in the later course of the sentence.

149. In continuing the manipulation of a Motive beyond the first
Imitation (the point at which the above examples were interrupted), the
possibilities are very numerous, and the greatest scope may be given to
the freedom of the writer's imagination and to his facility. Among
these, however, the following design is the most natural, and is commended to the beginner: After the first Imitation is finished, devote one
measure to a modulation into the Dominant key (or the relative key),
using lines which proceed as naturally as possible out of the preceding
measure, — *giving decided preference to sequential figures* (par. 95); then
make two announcements of the Motive in the new key. Thus, with the
first Motive (beginning in the middle of the second measure of Ex. 114):

Ex. 116.

Sequence.   Seq.

Episode : Modulation into D major.

New cont. associate.

Motive (in D).

Observe that the 2nd of these measures, devoted to the modulation, does not contain the entire Motive, but only figures from it, derived by sequence. *Such a passage is called an Episode.* Observe, further, that the sequences are not exact, and remember that such freedom is not only permissible, but necessary.

Notice how completely "new" the contrapuntal associate is, in the following measure, as compared with the first one; and notice how, *for variety*, this contrapuntal associate is *not* re-constructed, in the next measure, but corresponds to the preceding one.

Finally, observe how *d-sharp* is substituted for *d* at the beginning of the last measure, in order to introduce another modulation (this time into the relative key, E minor).

150. The formation, and the length, of an Episode are entirely optional, excepting that it must be in close keeping with what has gone before. It must, — like the contrapuntal associate, — be a *perfectly natural continuation* of the foregoing lines (par. 146-5); and this may refer to the line of *either the upper or the lower part.* For this reason, sequential formation is the most desirable.

151. Further, the continuation of Motive 2 (beginning with the 3rd measure of Ex. 115) might be about as follows:

Motive (in A minor).

Analyze carefully, and observe the agreement of this design with the suggestion given in par. 149.

152. The observant student will probably realize that a great part of the object and the labor of this method of composition centres in the formation of the *contrapuntal associates*, or of the "counterpoint" in general; and this is a task for which the past lessons in counterpoint must have prepared him. The difference between the preceding Exercises and the counterpoints shown in this lesson appears much greater than it actually is; it is merely a difference in rhythmic appearance, and is not at all of an essential character. Close comparison with the rules and illustrations given in Chap. XIV will prove this. If any additional directions are necessary, they are comprised in the following general rule: Be sure that some good interval appears (or is understood) at the accents, and at strong beats in general; lead the two parts smoothly to these points, maintaining a uniform rhythmic effect, and alternating (or combining) the shorter note-values so as to obtain a good rhythmic form in *each separate part.* To test this rule, analyze the contrapuntal treatment of every measure in all of the Two-part Inventions of **Bach.**

153. In pursuing the development of the Motive still further, it will be necessary (before rounding off the complete sentence with a perfect cadence in the original key) to introduce a few more episodic passages, modulations, and imitations of the Motive. Some of these are necessary, and determinable; though, in general, the details may be chosen with considerable freedom, and will depend upon the fancy of the writer, or upon the specific nature of the Motive.

154. For the beginner, a schedule like the following (embracing the entire sentence) will prove most natural and effective:

1. The announcement of the Motive (in either part).
2. The imitation of the Motive in the octave, in the other part.
3. An episode of one or two measures, modulating to the Dominant key.
4. Two announcements of the Motive in this key (one in each part).
5. An episode of one or two measures, modulating into the Relative (major or minor) key.

6. One or two announcements of the Motive in that key (either part).

7. An episode, modulating into the Subdominant key (or its Relative).

8. One announcement of the Motive in that key (either part).

9. An episode, modulating back to the original key.

10. One or two announcements of the Motive in that key.

11. Episode, and perfect cadence.

NOTE. *Either 5 and 6, or 7 and 8, or all of these, may be omitted.*

For example, the development of Motive 1, given in Examples 114 and 116, may be continued thus, — recommencing with No. 5 of the above details (end of Ex. 116):

The student will do wisely to copy out Exs. 114, 116 and 118, consecutively, so that he can analyze the whole sentence without interruption.

Observe, at * in the first measure of Ex. 118, the imitating of a figure that is not in the Motive. Such episodic imitations are as valuable as those of the motive itself.

Observe, at N. B. in the same measure, the brief rests. Also in measure 6, before the entrance of the Motive.

Observe, at N. B. in the 5th measure (of Ex. 118), the *alteration of one of the intervals in the given Motive.* The upward leap of a 4th is changed to a leap of the 6th. *Such little changes are not only permissible, but desirable, from time to time.*

Observe, at N. B. in the 6th measure, that the Motive enters in the third beat, instead of at the beginning of the measure. This is called Imitation in Shifted Rhythm, and is permissible and effective, if carefully tested.

Observe, further, the addition of extra parts, and the duplication of the lower part in octaves, at the approach to the perfect cadence.

Analyze every detail, most minutely; especially the formation of the various contrapuntal associates, and the Episodes.

155. A sentence of this kind is generally known as an **Invention.**

EXERCISE 15.

MOTIVE-DEVELOPMENT IN TWO-PART COUNTERPOINT.

Manipulate each of the following Motives, in the manner explained above, according to the schedule given in par. 154, as small **INVENTION.**

Each Motive should be developed twice, completely; beginning with the upper part for the first solution, and with the lower for the second solution:

[A solution of No. 5 will be found in the Appendix, to which the student **may** refer, after having made his own version.]

Besides these, invent a number of original Motives, similar in character and length to the above (and to those of **Bach** in his "Inventions"), and manipulate them in the indicated manner.

* * *

156. Nothing remains to be said about two-part counterpoint. The fundamental conditions which govern the association of two contrapuntal parts have been amply explained and illustrated in the foregoing lessons. All the essential rules, and all the important methods of treatment, have been thoroughly rehearsed.

It rests now with the student to continue the exercise of these methods in his own way, inventing thematic melodies and motives, and supplying them with contrapuntal associates, in order to gain more complete technical facility.   This he should not fail to do.   For if it be true that technical facility is the first and really indispensable condition of fluent and effective expression (whether reproductive or productive), it is also true that two-part counterpoint constitutes the groundwork of all tone-association; and, therefore, its command is the fundamental preparation for every task in the fuller styles of harmonic and contrapuntal writing.   To the student who has learned to think and feel the simultaneous progression of two parts, who can carry two melodies side by side with perfect ease and consciousness, all combinations are possible; and their complete mastery is to him only a question of time and, of course, earnest effort.

*   *   *

For further details of the Invention, the student is referred to the Author's " Applied Counterpoint," Chapter V.

*   *   *

———

<h1 style="text-align:center">CHAPTER XVI.</h1>

<h2 style="text-align:center">THREE-PART HARMONY.</h2>

157.   The next step in contrapuntal study is the simultaneous treatment of three individual melodic parts.   Review par. 1.

158.   " Individual " these three parts must be, each by itself, to a certain extent; for the contrapuntal principle, as has been shown, does not rest upon mere duplication of parts, or " accompaniment."   It involves the association and interaction of *separately* correct and satisfactory melodic lines.   At the same time, this individuality of each of the parts must be controlled and limited by necessary consideration for the movements of the other parts, and *harmonious agreement of each with the others ;* their independence should consist solely in their personal melodic formation, as melodies, and must not lead to conflict of harmonic formation.   In a word, to repeat the fundamental definition, *the parts are to be melodically distinct, but harmonically unanimous.*

159.   This statement admits of but one construction, and that is, that a harmonic basis is necessary ; and that, therefore, the underlying chords must first be defined, from point to point, as a general guide (at least) to the melodic course which the parts are severally to pursue.

160.   Of the three parts, — coördinate though they will all be, — some one is likely to be the *Leader* for the time being.   The reasons for this will be understood when the time comes.   It may be (is almost certain to be) that the Leader is that one of the parts which has the Motive ;

or it may be, rather frequently, the uppermost part, which attracts attention because of its position ; or it will be the one that is engaged in carrying out some sequential design, which causes it to step into the foreground for a while. Be this as it may, the mind is inclined to give *momentary preference to some single line,* and to define the chords from that line (as, for instance, the upper line in Ex. 123).

161. Such " harmonizing " of a melodic phrase is subject to one sweeping rule :

A tone " may " be harmonized by any chord of which it is a component interval.

That is, the tone may appear as Root, Third, Fifth, possibly as Seventh or even Ninth of some chord ; as Seventh or Ninth, however, only when it moves stepwise downward, or in some other way that provides for its resolution.

162. Thus, the tone *C* may indicate, *in C major,* the following chords :

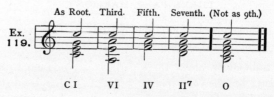

And, besides these, in its fuller significance, *in any key :*

163. This list is not exhaustive. The given tone may also appear as root, third, or fifth in several other chords of the seventh (as root, for instance, in the Dom.-7th chord of F major and minor, etc.).

The task of selecting the proper chord would be formidable, if this entire list of possibilities were always valid at every point. But the choice is very greatly reduced by the ruling key, or tonality; whether, for example, the *C* in Ex. 120 would be treated as a major third, or as a minor third, must depend upon whether it occurs in the neighborhood of A minor, or of A♭ major. And, consequently, the number of available chords for the harmonizing of the tone *C*, in C major or its vicinity, would dwindle down to the brief list given in Ex. 119.

Hence, further, while Ex. 120 discloses an inspiring outlook for the intelligent student, and clearly exhibits the infinitude of the composer's resources, it also suggests the necessity of rational limitation, and vindicates the truly vital principle of *tonality and key*, as temporary centralizing influences.

164. The same restrictions apply to every tone; as in the case of *C*, so with *D*, and the rest; among all the *possible* harmonizations there are a very few *probable* ones, to which preference must be given, and which are to be singled out as first choice.

Thus, the tone *D* suggests only the following chords, *in C major:*

Ex. 121.

As Root. Third. Fifth.

C II ⁶   ⁶₄   ₀V⁷ (VII) V ₆ V⁷   Not as 7th, or 9th.

The name ₀V⁷ means "Dominant-7th, Incomplete." The term "Incomplete" refers to the *omission of the root*. The name VII is not used in this book.

165. This more narrow, but more rational, choice of chords for each individual step of a scale, may be tabulated as follows, — for C major (or minor):

Ex. 122.

Step 1. Step 2. Step 3. Step 4. Step 5. Step 6. Step 7.

I	II	I	IV	V	(VI)	V
VI	V	(VI)	II	V⁷	IV	V⁷
IV	V⁷		V⁷	I	II	(III)
(II⁷)	Ex. 121.			(III)	V⁹	
Ex. 119.						

Compare Ex. 12 (par. 12).

Explanation. The first scale-step, of any key, may be harmonized either with the I, or VI, or IV (possibly the II⁷) of that key. The second step may be harmonized either with the II, or V, or V⁷ of that key. And so on.

Further, not only the fundamental form, but also the inverted forms of the chords may be used.

166. The application of this table to a given melodic succession, is made by simply defining, first, the *scale-step* which each melody-tone represents in the given key, and then selecting one from the group of chords that are valid for that scale-step.   For example : Given the melodic figure *e-d-c*, in C major ; these tones are steps 3-2-1, and may therefore be harmonized in the following ways (— as upper part, with a lower and one inner part) :

The above are all good.   Examine them carefully.   Many others are possible, especially by substituting other (inverted) forms of the same harmonic succession, — compare Nos. 4 and 5 ; or by modulating into related keys, as in Nos. 8 and 9.

The following are faulty :

In the first group, the successive 5ths (in the outer parts) result from two causes : first, from harmonizing step 3 with the VI (which is possible, but rare, according to the table in Ex. 122) ; and second, from the unnatural chord-succession, V into IV (see Ex. 125).   The latter succession is also responsible for the faults in the third and fourth groups.   In the second group there is an awkward chord-succession (II into IV, — Ex. 125).

167. From this it appears, that the choice of chords from the lists in Ex. 122 is somewhat limited by the rules of *natural chord-succession.*

Of these rules the student may be already aware. If so, he might omit the next few paragraphs (up to and including par. 176).

168. It is true, ultimately, that any chord-succession may be employed, — when the student shall have learned to overcome awkward conditions by perfectly correct contrapuntal movements (correct *melodic* movement in every part). But the beginner must respect the following distinctions.

Some chord-successions are natural, corroborating the conditions created by the relations of the chords to each other, and to their Tonic centre. Others are more or less unnatural and awkward.

169. The following table shows how each one of the six triads may progress ; that is, which chords may come *after* each :

After the I, — any chord of the same key or of any other key.

After the V, — either the I, or the VI (which is the " parallel " triad of the I). Possibly the III.

After the IV, any chord excepting the III.

After the II, — either the V (a perfect 5th below), or the VI (a perfect 5th above).

After the VI, — any chord excepting the I (which is its own " parallel chord " and therefore should not follow, but *precede*, the inferior one).

After the III, — either the IV, or the VI.

For every one of these movements (and prohibitions) there are satisfactory scientific reasons. This, however, is not the place for their demonstration. *The student must know the facts*, and must therefore memorize the tables, and embrace every opportunity of putting them into practice, until they become a second nature to him. If his musical instinct is quick, his mind will all the more readily assent to them. If not, he will have to work a little harder.

170. Stated inversely, the following are the chord-progressions *which should be avoided :*

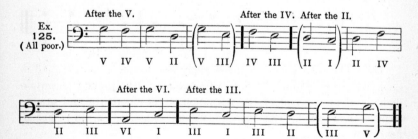

The succession V–III is really good; but the III is a rare chord, and should be avoided, as a rule. The succession II–I is stiff, but not bad; it is always possible *when inverted forms are used,* — that is, when the chord-3rd, or 5th, appears in the lowermost part, instead of the Root.

171. Every one of the above unnatural chord-progressions can be used, *when the second one of the two chords is inverted.* For example, the V may be followed by an *inversion* of the IV, or of the II.

172. This refers principally to the *first* inversion, — the chord of the 6th, which is almost invariably good.

The second inversion of any triad-form (the $\frac{6}{4}$ chord) is rare and hazardous. It would be wise for the student to avoid all $\frac{6}{4}$ chords, *excepting the second inversion of the I, and of the IV* . These are good.

In other words, avoid the chord-fifth in the lower part, excepting in the I and IV.

173. For $\frac{6}{4}$ chords, the following rules must be observed:

Leaps are not good, either to or from a $\frac{6}{4}$ chord (in the lower part) ; excepting, as usual, during chord-repetition.

Six-four chords should not occur in direct succession.

For illustration, this lower part is faulty:

Ex. 126.   etc.

On the contrary, the following is good:

Ex. 127.

174. The rules given for the V apply also to the V^7 and V^9 (and to their Incomplete forms, $_0V^7$ and $_0V^9$) ; but more strictly, and with certain limitations, on account of the resolution of the chord-7th and 9th, — stepwise downward. (See par. 58, second clause, — Ex. 49.) For illustration :

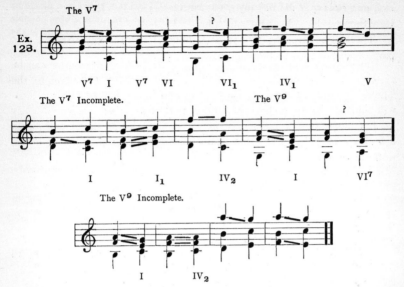

Group 3 is doubtful, because of the *inverted form of the VI.* That triad is very rarely inverted. In group 4, the seventh of the chord (*f* in the upper part) remains where it is ; this is always good, if the proper resolution follows. As already stated, the term "Incomplete" signifies that the Root is omitted.

175. The II⁷ is treated like the V⁷. Like the II, it passes into the V, or into *inverted* forms of the I.

The other chords of the Seventh seldom occur as essential bodies, but often as descending passing-notes. Thus :

176. All of these rules apply, as usual, *to the minor mode*, precisely as to major. The only modification is the occasional *lowering of the 7th scale-*

step, and raising of the 6th step, according to par. 32 (Ex. 30), which review thoroughly.   See also par. 184.

Transpose Exs. 123 to 130 to C minor, — at the keyboard, — with particular reference to these paragraphs (32 and 184).

177.   In this lesson, the student will confine his exercises to the " good " chords (review par. 12, Ex. 12), and to one key at a time.   This will simplify the use of Ex. 122, and of par. 169.

For illustration, a melodic sentence in C major as upper part; *each tone an essential chord-tone* (that is, no passing-notes or neighboring notes, in these lessons) :

N. B.   In measure 1, beat 3, the *d* is doubled and *f* is omitted.   On the next beat, the chord-5th *g* is omitted.   In measure 2, beat 3, *e* is doubled and *g* omitted. On the next beat, *g* is again omitted.   In measure 3, beat 1, *d* is omitted.

In all of these cases, enough of the chord is present to define it beyond doubt; the object of the omissions is, simply, to obtain the best melodic progressions.

Either of the three endings is good.

178.   This is, to be sure, a purely *harmonic* task; merely the defining of the chords that are required or suggested by the successive melody-tones.   But it acquires a certain contrapuntal flavor through the effort to give each separate part a good melodic form.   This can be done by judicious choice of duplication, and of omission, in the spelling of the chords, as seen in Ex. 130.   Sing, or play, or write out, each of the above three parts alone by itself, and it will be seen that something more is accomplished than the mere harmonic accompaniment of the given melody. Such practice is so beneficial, so instructive and so stimulating, that the student should make extremely thorough use of it, before undertaking the genuine contrapuntal treatment of three parts.

EXERCISE 16.

THREE HARMONIC PARTS, AS MELODIC HARMONIZATION. PRIMARY CHORDS.

Harmonize each of the following melodies, as upper part, *with "good" chords only*, — the I, V, IV, V^7 and V^9, — as shown in Ex. 130.

Each melody in the same key throughout.

Endeavor to make each part, separately, as melodious as possible.

If the melody is high, one staff will suffice (as in Ex. 128); if low, two staves will be more convenient. Or, in any case, the student may use two staves, if he so desires.

Several versions (at least three) of each melody should be made.

[A solution of Melody 6 will be found in the Appendix.]

CHAPTER XVII.

SECONDARY CHORDS.

179. For the employment of the other, comparatively inferior (but decidedly useful and effective) chords, the tables in Ex. 122, and par. 169, must be applied in their fullest significance.

180. The best of these chords are the II and its first inversion, and the II[7] and its inversions. They harmonize steps 4 and 2.

The VI is used chiefly as substitute for the I, after the V or V[7]. *It is not inverted;* that is, the Root always appears in the lower part, — excepting in the succession of 6ths, shown in Ex. 132. It harmonizes step 1, — rarely step 3.

The III is *very rare.* It harmonizes step 7 when it *descends,* stepwise, to step 6.

181. The following groups illustrate certain specific applications:

Ex. 131.

II V[7] VI   II V   V V III II[7]

To these, add Ex. 129, which was not used in the preceding lesson.

In group 1, the VI appears after the V[7]. In group 2, the first version is better than the second one, because it is always better to *change the chord* at the bar, if possible. In group 3, the III appears as harmonization of the *descending 7th scale-step* (in the line 8-7-6). The treatment of the Sevenths is shown in Ex. 129, which review.

182. Successive first inversions (chords of the 6th) are always good; especially when used in stepwise progression. Thus:

Ex. 132.

6 6 6 6 6 6 6 6 6 6 6 6

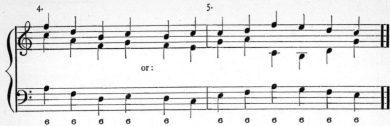

Group 1 is better than group 2; the effect is more compact when the inner part lies closer to the upper one.   Group 3 is also good.   Group 5 exhibits an unusually long line of sixths; it is good, because of the uniform parallelism of the outer parts; compare par. 107, last sentence.   But observe the conduct of the inner part, which redeems its independence by occasional contrary motion, and wide skips.

183.   In sequential successions, almost any irregularity is excused, as usual. See par. 29.   For example, in the following, many of the conditions of par. 169 are set aside.   It is mainly necessary that the first figure is regular (normal), *and that it interlocks readily with the first tone of its sequence,* in each part.

For illustration :

N. B. The uppermost slurs indicate the actual figure and its sequences. The inner and lower slurs are merely noted to show *how the sequence interlocks* with its (preceding) figure. Examine every group very carefully, observing exactly the effect of each system of slurs.

Any good figure will yield a number of sequences, but the points at which the sequence may *begin* must be those into which the figure itself runs smoothly.

184. In Minor, the difficulties of good melodic movement are increased, especially in sequences. The notes of the major versions need never be changed, but *the notation of steps 6 and 7* may need to be modified by accidentals. As a rule, *whenever step 7 descends*, it must be written *b-flat* (in C minor). And *where step 6 ascends*, it must be *a-natural* (in C minor).

Transpose all of the above examples (131, 132, 133) to C minor, — both as written exercise, and at the keyboard; and closely observe the application of this rule. *Do this without fail.* First review, thoroughly, Ex. 30, and observe that the present rule is more sweeping than that of the melodic minor scale.

EXERCISE 17.

THREE HARMONIC PARTS. PRIMARY AND SECONDARY CHORDS. SEQUENCES.

Harmonize the following melodies, with the material of this chapter. Review the directions given in Exercise 16. Use two staves.

2.
4.
7 6
II1 6 4
VI
II 6 4
VI
5.
6 4
6 4
6.
II 6 4
7.
7 6
6 4
8.
7 6
II7
6 4
9. Successive 6ths.
6 6 6 6 6 6
10.
7 6
6 6 6
6 6 6 6
6 4
VI
7 6
II
11. Sequences.
6 6 6

12.

[A solution of Melody 8 will be found in the Appendix.]

Besides these, the student may re-harmonize the melodies of Exercise 16, introducing Secondary chords where possible.

Also write a number of original three-part sentences, like the above, with Sequences, and with Successive 6ths.

CHAPTER XVIII.

WITH MODULATIONS.

185. The rules for changing the key are all given in par. 81, par. 86, par. 88 and par. 90. Review the whole of Chapter VIII, but very particularly the paragraphs mentioned.

186. As usual:

1. The keys which occur transiently in a sentence should be *next-related* to the principal key.

2. The key may always be changed easily, after some form of the *Tonic harmony* has completed the momentary key.

3. But *chromatic* modulations may be made at any point, — if the chromatic succession itself is properly prepared. And the presence of the chromatic progression excuses almost any irregularity.

187. The first melody of Exercise 17 may also be harmonized as follows, with transient changes of key:

Ex. 134.

188. When the chromatic progression occurs in the given melody itself, it may generally be treated in one of these two ways:

point, — if the chromatic
succession itself is
properly prepared
And the presence of
the chromatic
progression excuses

almost any irregularity

'88.   When the chromatic
progression occurs
in the given melody
itself, it may
generally be treated
in one of these two ways

Chapter 18.

1. The keys which occur transiently in a sentence should be next related to the principal key.

2. The key may always be changed easily after some form of the Tonic harmony has completed the momentary key.

3. But chromatic modulation may be made at any

1. The first of the two chromatic tones may be harmonized with a triad, and the second tone with a Dom.-7th chord, or diminished-7th chord.   Or,

2. Each tone may be harmonized with some chord of the 6th (confirming par. 182).

For illustration :

Ex. 135.

In the first version, the transient keys are not all next-related to the original key ; nor does the melody end in the latter. The *chromatic* character of the harmony accounts for all this.   See pars. 88 and 89.   Also glance at the Notes to Ex. 158, *a.*

In the second version, the lines of chromatic 6ths are so indefinite that it is scarcely possible to prove the keys. They are, properly speaking, no more than *passing chords*, and do not actually change the key, which remains C major throughout. At the same time, any of the intimated keys might be confirmed at once, *by resolving the chord* in some legitimate manner; this would, of course, change the melody at that point. For instance, version 2 may *end* like version 1, by simply resolving the last chord of the third measure as Incomplete Dom.-7th of B minor.

189.   Closely allied to this principle of very transient modulations (shown in version 2 of Ex. 135), is the common practice of momentarily *altering certain Scale-steps* by accidentals.   This gives the *chord* a so-called " altered " form ; but does not change the *key.*

190.   Of many possible Altered scale-steps, the following are the most frequent and effective :

1. The *lowered 6th Scale-step, in major.*

2. The *raised 4th Scale-step, both in major and in minor.*

For illustration (in C major) :

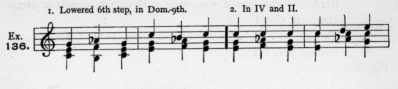

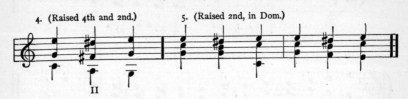

Observe that a *Tonic* chord always follows the altered one, as resolution, and in confirmation of the principal key.

Observe that by lowering the 6th scale-step the *chord of the diminished-7th becomes valid for major* (as well as minor).

Observe that the raised 4th step occurs only in the II, IV, II⁷, IV⁷ (Subdominant chords). Also that it may be accompanied by the raised 2nd step,—in the II. And that the raised 2nd step may occur *alone*,—in the V or V⁷.

Further, the raised 4th scale-step in minor :

Ex. 137.

Observe that, here again, the raised 4th step occurs only in Subdominant chords (II–IV–II⁷–IV⁷).

Observe also, that the *Tonic* chord usually follows, as resolution,—though it is perfectly proper to pass from *these* altered chords into a Dominant chord (measure 2), because the latter naturally moves at once into the desired Tonic.

191. The lowering of the 7th scale-step, and raising of the 6th, *in minor,* — of which such extended use has been made in all the minor Exercises, — is nothing more than an application of the same principle of "Altered" scale-steps. See, again, par. 32 (Ex. 30), par. 184, and the following :

192. In minor, it is also possible to lower the 2nd Scale-step, but only in the II (usually in its chord of the 6th). Thus:

EXERCISE 18.

MODULATIONS, AND ALTERED STEPS.

Harmonize the following melodies, introducing changes of key wherever possible or desirable, according to the above rules. Use two staves, as a rule. In the first six melodies, the * indicates where modulations are to be made.

[A solution of Melody 7 will be found in the Appendix.]

Besides these, write a number of original three-part sentences, like the above, with modulations and altered chords.

CHAPTER XIX.

CONTRAPUNTAL HARMONY.

193. The consideration of melodic independence in the several parts becomes more emphatic when the same given melody is adopted, alternately, as *inner* and as *lower* part.

The task differs but little from that of the preceding chapters. It is still the act of harmonization, and subject to almost exactly the same rules as before. But the attention is necessarily more evenly divided between the parts, and the *melodic* nature of the exercise is sufficiently emphasized to justify the designation " contrapuntal harmony."

194. In the following, the given melody is placed in the upper part, and harmonized as before ; possibly with somewhat greater concern for the melodic movements of the other parts :

Ex. 140.

It is significant, that the two outer parts alone, without the inner, form a perfectly satisfactory counterpoint in this example.

195. When the given melody is placed in the inner part, the chords are defined according to former tables (Ex. 122, and par. 169), — though there may be greater freedom in the choice.

The tones required to complete the chosen chords are so divided between the outer parts as to give good *melodic* results in both. This is especially necessary in the upper part. The lower part is, of course, subject to the rules of chord-inversion. Review, carefully, par. 173, and Ex. 126 (in which the above given melody appears in the inner part).

For example :

Ex. 141.

Here, the inner and upper parts yield good counterpoint, without the **lower.**

196. When the given melody is placed in the lower part, the chords, again, are defined according to the tables, — but somewhat more strictly. For the lower part, the table of Ex. 122 should be thus modified:

Applied to the above given melody, the result might be:

In the first of these versions, the two outer parts give a good counterpoint, without the inner.

In the second version, the inner and lower might stand alone, without the upper.

These facts are significant, in each of the above examples, and almost suggest the feasibility of counterpointing first one part alone against the given part, and then adding the third part. It is left to the student to experiment in his own way.

Transpose Examples 140, 141 and 143 to *C minor*, at the keyboard, — with reference to par. 184.

*   *   *

197. After the simple harmonic outline has been fixed in this manner, it may be *amplified and embellished by accelerating the rhythmic movement to two, three, or four notes to each beat.*

The process is the same as defined in par. 74, par. 92, par. 105, par. 111, par. 113, par. 117, par. 119 and par. 121, all of which must first be thoroughly reviewed.

198. But the quicker rhythmic movement is not to be maintained (constantly) in any single part. It must appear in *alternating parts,* as shown in Examples 66, 76, 108, 109, — which must also be reviewed. See also Ex. 111.

199. This manipulation of the original essential tones is not only desirable, but absolutely necessary; and the student must not consider the task of 3-part contrapuntal harmony fulfilled until he has so accustomed himself to the addition of unessential (embellishing) tones, that they will naturally suggest themselves at once, and even assist, or influence, the choice of the essential tones.

200. For illustration, Ex. 140 may be accelerated to a rhythm of two notes to each beat in alternating parts, about as follows :

Ex. 144.

Compare this very carefully with the original form (Ex. 140); and endeavor to obtain other solutions.

N. B. Observe that the rhythm of the *upper part* is always regular; that is, *the quicker tones are applied in the upper part at the unaccented beats.* This is desirable in the upper part only, because of its melodic prominence; it does not apply at all to the inner, or lower, part.

It is, of course, also possible to quicken the rhythm of a simple three-part harmonic sentence to two notes to each beat, by shifting either one of the three parts forward, — as shown in Chap. X. See Exs. 78, 79, 80. This should not be considered as a valuable or effective resource, and its use, unless very moderate, is not commended. Still, when applied in *alternating* parts, as in Ex. 81; or with occasional *rests,* as in Ex. 89; — it may be permissible, especially at single points, where no other form of amplification seems convenient. Thus, with Ex. 140:

Further, the same model (Ex. 140) accelerated to three notes to each beat in alternating parts :

Manipulate this in other ways. Observe, again, the regular rhythmic treatment of the *upper part.*

Further, with four notes to each beat :

Par. 75.   Par. 121.

Compare this *carefully* with Ex. 140, and observe the degree of liberty that is taken with the original.   Again, note the rhythm of the *upper part*.

Also, make a number of other versions.

Also, review par. 184, and transpose all the above to C minor.

EXERCISE 19.

CONTRAPUNTAL THREE-PART HARMONY.

1. Manipulate Examples 141 and 143 in amplified rhythms of two, then three, and then four notes to each beat, — as shown in Exs. 144, 145, and 146.

2. Harmonize each of the following given melodies in the three ways illustrated in Exs. 140, 141 and 143; — first as upper part, where it is written; then as inner part, one octave lower than written; and then as lower part, two octaves lower than written (possibly a little less than two octaves, transposed to another key).   An *occasional* eighth-note may be used, as broken beat, even in these original essential harmonic versions, in any part, to facilitate the melodic movements.

Bb major.

3. Each of these simple harmonic versions is then to be manipulated in rhythms of 2, 3 and 4 notes to each beat, as indicated above.

[A partial solution of Melody 3 will be found in the Appendix.]

4. Select a large number of finished sentences from Exercises 16, 17 and 18, and amplify them, similarly, to the quicker rhythmic forms shown in Exs. 144, 145 and 146.

CHAPTER XX.

THREE-PART COUNTERPOINT.

201. In the four preceding lessons, the association of three melodic parts was explained and conducted on the basis of the *chords* which the individual tones of one given melodic line suggested or required.

202. This is, strictly speaking, the only correct manner, at least for the determination of all the fundamental conditions; because it is the **Chords** which constitute the proper basis of all harmonious music. The inharmonious effects which are more or less plentifully interspersed, in an effective and interesting musical sentence, are merely modifications or embellishments of the chords, and neither can nor should be accounted for in any other way. No matter how freely the dissonant particles are intermingled, the *general* impression must be an harmonious one; for no music may be called good, or may be expected to produce an agreeable and acceptable impression, unless it is harmonious as a whole. Inharmonious music is really not music at all, in in the sense in which our reason, our instincts, and the judgment of the whole civilized world, compel us to regard it. The chords are the "accordant" tone-bodies, which guarantee this necessary prevalence of harmonious effect. And therefore the association of parts, even when individual and melodically independent of each other (as is the case in genuine counterpoint) must be determined, fundamentally, by reference to the chords.

203. But there are other modes of arriving at a good harmonious result, more distinctively contrapuntal in character than the simple harmonization of the given melody. When the student has cultivated his sense of chord-succession sufficiently, and has reached that stage of progress at which the chords have become a part of his nature, and perform their functions automatically, he will find it possible and natural to centre his attention upon the *melodic* movements of the parts, and will achieve a good result more quickly and surely from this point of view.

204. In *genuine* counterpoint it is not the movements of the chords, but the movements of the *separate tones,* that create the required impression. The influence of the chords is felt rather than heard. In the above examples *there are too many chord-changes, at regular intervals ;* as a rule, there is a different chord for each beat, and therefore the chord-movements are too frequent and obtrusive. This is probably the most obvious defect in such harmonic sentences ; under such conditions a genuine contrapuntal effect cannot easily be gained, — not even when copious inharmonic embellishing tones are added (as in Exs. 144, 145 and 146).

205. The most effectual method of diminishing such persistent chord-impressions, and increasing the significance of the tone-lines as such, is *to dwell longer upon each single chord,* or, at least, upon certain (strong) chords ; and, in general, *to vary the length of the chords.* While the chord is stationary (or passive), the separate parts are unhampered, and can move about with greater freedom. (This is shown in Ex. 148.)

206. In these unrestrained melodic movements, the parts hold each other in check, to some extent, not only by mutual agreement with the underlying chord, but by *harmony of movement among themselves.* This latter element is of extreme importance, especially in elementary counterpoint, and manifests itself most frequently in the following two forms :

   1. Parallel 3rds, or parallel 6ths, between any two of the parts.
   2. Duplication of any 3-tone stepwise figure, in the opposite direction.

For example :

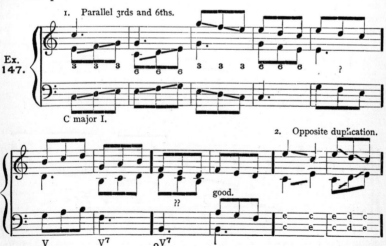

In the first measure, the inner and lower parts run parallel in 3rds; in the next measure, in 6ths. *The chord remains unchanged.* In the third measure, it is the outer parts; in the fourth measure, the upper and inner. The fifth measure is harsh, because both parts clash with the chord-3rd (*e*), which is a poor interval to double. Measure eight is still worse, because of the collision with the leading-tone (*b*).

In the second example, the tones *e-c*, or *e-d-c*, are counterpointed in "opposite duplication" by *c-e*, *c-d-e*. Occasional evidences of these almost inevitable coöperations will be found in Exs. 144, 145 and 146.

207. The employment of these two convenient (and almost invariably acceptable and effective) figures, in the *prolongation of good chords*, yields a great variety of forms, with genuine contrapuntal result. For illustration:

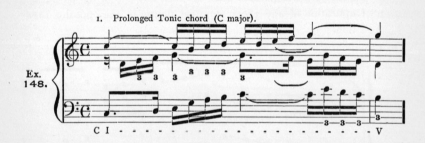

3. Ditto.

C I - - - - - - - - - - (IV) - - - - - - V⁷

4. Prolonged Dominant chord.

C (I)   V - - - - (II⁷) - - - - - - - - - - - - - I

Observe that the prolongation of the chord extends exactly to the end of some measure, so that the change of harmony occurs *at an accent*, and thus confirms the rhythm. This is important.

Observe, also, that in a few cases the current of the moving parts seems to denote, transiently, some other (related) chord, — indicated in parenthesis.

208. In the following three complete sentences, a number of note-worthy modulatory incidents appear :

1. *Andante.*

Ex. 149.

C I ——— IV   (VI) II ——— V ——— I   (IV)   VI

II⁷   V⁷ I———   dV⁷   I V———   D———

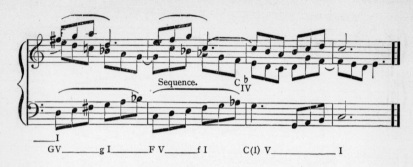

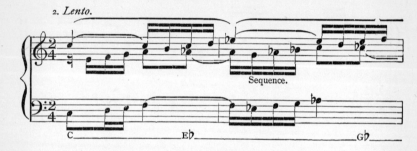

Explanation. No. 1 contains the so-called "Exchange of Mode"; — in measure 6, fifth beat, the *f-sharp* in the upper part changes the mode from *d* minor to *D* major; in the next measure, the *b-flat* changes the expected *G* major to *g* minor; and in the following measure the *a-flat* changes the expected *F* major to *f* minor. The same exchange occurs in No. 2, measure 6 (from the expected *g* minor to *G* major).

Such a substitution of major for minor, or of minor for major, is possible at almost any point,—particularly after any dominant chord, which resolves into either the major or minor tonic.

In No. 1, with this exception, the keys are all properly interrelated. On the last beat of the 8th measure, the *a-flat* (lower part) becomes the lowered 6th scale-step of C major.

In No. 2, on the other hand, the successive keys are quite foreign to each other (excepting near the end, where, as is rational, the modulatory movements concentrate toward the principal keynote). These irregular modulations are chiefly accounted for by the *chromatic progressions ;* in measure three, by the enharmonic agreement of *g-flat* with *f-sharp.* But the factor most actively engaged in these changes is the so-called " Pivotal tone," — that is, a tone which, being common to two keys (sometimes in a widely different capacity), is used as a point of contact, or *pivot,* upon which to swing the melodic movements from the one key over into the other. Thus, in measure three (of No. 2) the *g-flat* (lower part), as keynote of *G*-flat, is made identical with *f-sharp,* as leading-tone of *g* minor. At the end of the measure, this same *f-sharp* becomes the raised 4th scale-step of *C.* In measure five, the *g* (upper part), which was the 4th step of *d* minor, is held as keynote of *G,* and then becomes the leading-tone of *A*-flat major. The same operation may be claimed for several other changes of key, — as for instance, in measure one, the *c* (as keynote of *C*) becoming the 6th scale-step of *E*-flat major ; in measure six, the *b* (lower part), as 3rd step of *G,* becoming the leading-tone of C ; in measure four, the *e* (inner part), as 3rd step of *C,* becoming the 2nd step of *d* minor, — and so on.

This principal of pivotal (or common) tones is very prevalent, and very effective, in modulation, — but it must be applied with caution, *under the smoothest possible melodic conditions.*

Number 3 is not to be taken too seriously. It represents the utmost extreme to which *free chromatic movements* may be carried, and reflects an attitude towards Tone-relationships that, despite its popularity in modern music, is decidedly hazardous for the student. *In moderation,* such hazy delineations are surely permissible, but the beginner has no motive whatever for their employment. At the same time, he should devote some little attention to this style, and may experiment with it.

There are four qualities whose presence, and careful consideration, make No. 3 justifiable : First, very smooth melodic movements, almost constantly, — relieved here and there by a skip along some good chord-line ; second, *there is some good chord-form at almost every accent, some harmonic tone-cluster towards which the parts unanimously lead* (as shown by the letters beneath the staff, the chord-*names* being left to the student's analysis) ; third, there are sufficient sequences and other evidences of consistent formation, and agreement among the melodic figures used, to prevent the sentence from being senseless and purposeless ; fourth, from time to time there is a *regular resolution of a Dom.-chord into its Tonic.* The more of these the better, as they effectually prevent eccentricity.

Observe, in all three examples, the frequent application of the devices given in par. 206 (Ex. 147).

Observe, also, how flexible and smooth the melodic movements constantly are,— *especially at the bars.*

Analyze every tone, most thoroughly.

209. Sentences of such free modulatory character may be somewhat beyond the reach of the elementary student. But this freedom may be attained by earnest and thorough practice. Not at once. The student must exercise the simpler forms at first, so long and so exhaustively that the voices begin to acquire life and freedom from within, and seem to move of their own volition. That facility once gained, the more ample and excursive movements will naturally follow. Hand in hand with this long course of faithful practice must go the exhaustive analysis of contrapuntal masterworks, — at present, passages with two, and with three, individual melodic lines.

EXERCISE 20.

THREE-PART COUNTERPOINT.

1. To the following melody, as *upper* part, add an inner and a lower part, in similar rhythm (uniform 8ths):

2. To the following melody, as *inner* part, add an upper and a lower part, in similar rhythm:

3. To the following melody, as *lower* part, add an inner and an upper part, in similar rhythm.

[The solution of these three sentences will be found in the Appendix, to which reference may be made after the student has exhausted his ingenuity in solving them himself.]

4. Write a number of *brief* exercises, applying the devices of par. 206, as shown in Ex. 148.

5. Write a number of original sentences in the style of Ex. 149,— especially No. 1.

CHAPTER XXI.

MOTIVE-DEVELOPMENT.

210. The application of the elements of three-part counterpoint to the manipulation of a Motive, is conducted in practically the same manner as was shown in Chapter XV, with reference to two-part counterpoint. That chapter should first be thoroughly reviewed.

211. The character of the motive is not materially affected by the number of contrapuntal parts employed, excepting that it may be a trifle more serious and rhythmically subdued for three parts than for two. Consequently, almost any of the motives given in Exercise 15 may be utilized here, in slightly moderated tempo, for illustrating the methods of manipulation in a contrapuntal association of three parts.

212. The motive may be first announced in either the upper, inner, or lower part ; but its first *imitation* should follow in the next higher or lower one.

The most effective and most frequent practice is to place the first imitation of the motive in the *Dominant key* (that is, each tone a perfect fifth higher, or a perfect fourth lower, than in the preceding announcement).

The next imitation (the third announcement) is then made again in the original key, usually an octave higher or lower than at first.

During these imitations of the motive, the other part, or parts, continue their melodic movements, as usual, according to the rules of counterpoint with which the student is familiar. For example, with the first motive given in Chapter XV (Ex. 113), beginning in the lower part :

The motive is first announced in the lower part, and ends upon the first (accented) beat of the second measure. The imitation, assigned to the next higher (inner) part, enters somewhat abruptly, inasmuch as it instantly denotes the change of key — to the Dominant. (There are various ways of avoiding such an abrupt entrance of a new part, when sufficiently rude to require modification; the best of these is illustrated in Ex. 151.)

During this second announcement of the motive, the lower part continues, of course, as ordinary contrapuntal associate.

The third announcement of the motive occurs in the remaining (upper) part, an octave higher than at first; the two other parts meanwhile run on without interruption, forming an association of three contrapuntal melodies.

213. Any such abrupt entrance of the first imitation of the Motive as was seen in the inner part (Ex. 150), may be mollified by *adding a beat or two* to the first part (the Motive itself). In the above case, it is best to add two beats, so that the final tone in that part is merely shifted to the *next accent*. These beats are so employed as to effect the modulation into the new key. See Ex. 151, second measure.

214.   Such additional (or " intermediate ") tones may be affixed to the first announcement of the Motive, without injuring or obscuring the latter, if they are chosen in strict conformity with its general melodic and rhythmic character ; and if they are carried to the next accent only, so that nothing more than an exchange of accents takes place.

In small measures ($\frac{2}{4}$, $\frac{3}{4}$, $\frac{3}{8}$, etc.), the intermediate tones will equal a full measure ; in larger ones (as $\frac{4}{4}$, $\frac{6}{8}$, etc.), they will equal a half-measure.

Such interlined, or added, beats come under the head of *episodic* tones.   See the explanatory Notes to Ex. 116.

215.   In the following manipulation of the same motive, intermediate tones are added to the Motive itself, as a brief episode, or interlude ; and a similar episode is added to the Imitation.   *Both of these serve as modulations*, to prepare for the transposed imitations : —

Compare the last measure, here, with that of Ex. 150. See par. 207 (Ex. 148).

216. The three-part counterpoint, which results from adding the third announcement of the Motive to the two preceding parts, and which is to continue more or less constantly to the end of the sentence, does not differ in any essential respect from the exercises of the foregoing chapter. Here, as there, the vital requirement is *to secure some good chord-form at the accents* or principal beats, and to lead each one of the three parts smoothly and melodiously from one of these chord-nodes to the next.

This does not mean that the chord-form must actually *appear*, at each accent. It is quite necessary to disguise it somewhat, by ties (suspensions) or passing-tones, — as seen in many places in Ex. 149 (for instance, in No. 1, measures 7 and 10). But the harmonious cluster must be perfectly evident.

217. To this fundamental rule, one other may be added: It is absolutely necessary to restrain the rhythmic movements of one and another of the three parts (alternately), in order to avoid rhythmic confusion, and too much commotion. Very rarely indeed should all three parts at once run in rapid rhythm (for instance, four notes to a beat); at least one of the parts should move at a quieter pace than the others; — this may be *any* part, and should frequently interchange with the others.

For the same reason, *rests* should occasionally be used; and from time to time one or another of the parts should be silent for a measure or more. Further : Free use should be made of the two devices indicated in par. 206.

218. The validity of these essential rules may be tested by careful analysis of the three-part Inventions of Bach. For example, the first ten measures of Invention No. 10 ; the first six measures of No. 14 ; the first six measures of No. 12 ; the first seven measures of No. 8 ; the first seven measures of No. 3 ; the first five measures of No. 1.

In analyzing these passages from the beginning of the three-part Inventions, the student will observe that the design suggested in the above examples (with reference to the treatment of the Motive) is followed in a general way, but with considerable freedom.   He will notice that Bach usually announces his Motive first in the upper or inner part, and that the lower part accompanies it from the start, in somewhat free contrapuntal association; further, that his Motives are often longer than the above; and that frequent episodic "interludes" are introduced between the announcements of the Motive.   The more carefully and extensively the student prosecutes the important study of analysis, the more he will see and learn.

219.   The development of a Motive into a complete sentence is conducted with three contrapuntal parts in the same general manner as with two.   The complete schedule is given in par. 154, which the student is advised to adopt, with such modifications (omissions or additions) as the increased number of parts, or his own purpose, may dictate.

Applied to the first Motive of Exercise 15, the result might be about as follows :

Analyze this (first without, and then with, the keyboard) most thoroughly, and observe the following noteworthy traits:

The free (or auxiliary) bass at the beginning, as associate of the first presentation of the Motive.

In measures 8 and 9 (lower part), the prolongation of the first tone of the Motive. This occurs frequently, and is owing to the fact that the Motive begins with the 5th scale-step (5th of the tonic harmony), which requires caution when in the lower part (par. 173).

In measure 17, the slight alteration of the Motive (upper part); also in measure 19; and in measure 22 (lower part).

In measures 19, 20 and 21, the episode, based upon the peculiar rhythmic treatment of the repeated figure in the inner part. At the same time, the silence of the lower part for a whole measure; a few measures later again, and longer.

The brief rest in measure 22 (inner part), and later, in each part.

In measure 20, the distinct *perfect cadence* (in *D* minor). This is important.

In measures 34 and 35, the *crossing* of the upper and inner parts. This is permissible, if the lines are not too long (or too completely) obscured.

In the final measure, the cadence in G *major.* See explanatory Notes to Ex. 149, first clauses.

The frequent slurs, which everywhere indicate some linear purpose, — usually the closer interaction of the several parts, by fragmentary imitation.

EXERCISE 21.

Motive–Development, with Three Contrapuntal Parts.

Continue Ex. 151 and develop the given Motive to a complete Invention (similar to the general design and method of Ex. 152).

2. Make another complete solution of the Motive manipulated in Ex. 152, beginning with the lower (or inner) part.

3. Manipulate each of the following Motives, in the manner above shown. Each Motive may (and should) be developed in three wholly different ways, beginning respectively with the upper part (for the first announcement of the Motive), then beginning with the inner part, — and then with the lower. The key may be altered, if necessary, to secure the proper register, *and invite a different train of thought for each solution.*

N. B. The student should make free use of all the devices and licenses suggested in Ex. 152, and of any others that his ingenuity may prompt; avoiding *too close* adherence to any of the given "rules," but always assuring himself, conscientiously, that he is obtaining a perfectly natural and harmonious product, and guarding scrupulously against eccentricity, or extravagance of any kind.

1. *Allegretto.*　　2. *Lento.*

Interlude.

3. *Allegro moderato.*

4. *Andante.*

Optional.

[A solution of Motive 6 will be found in the Appendix, to which the student may refer after completing his own version.]

4. Manipulate, with three contrapuntal parts, some (or all) of the Motives given in Exercise 15: numbers 2, 3, 5, 6, 10 and 11 are recommended for this purpose.

5. Besides these, the student may invent a number of original Motives, similar in character and length to the above, and develop them as usual. In that case, the music is *all* his own.

*　　*　　*

For further details of the Invention with three parts, the student is referred to the author's "Applied Counterpoint," Chapters VI and VII.

*　　*　　*

CHAPTER XXII.

FOUR-PART HARMONY.

220. The fundamental harmonic conditions are not affected by the number of parts.

The association of four parts is subject to precisely the same rules as govern the association of three, as far as the choice of chords is concerned. Therefore, the tables given in Chapter XVI (Ex. 122 and par. 169) are valid for the present tasks.

221. The chief difference between three-part and four-part harmony is that in the latter the parts are somewhat more crowded, and are therefore more restricted in their individual melodic movements, — especially the two inner parts; the compass of each part is narrower, and the progressions smoother and quieter than when only three parts are used.

Further, there are fewer omissions, and more duplications of the chord-intervals.

222. As a rule, the best tone to double is the root of the chord.

But it is always correct to double one of the good scale-steps, namely, steps 1, 5 and 4; excepting when these chance to be the dissonant interval of the chord (the chord-7th or chord-9th, neither of which should be doubled).

It is almost always wrong to double the 7th scale-step (the leading-tone).

In the six-four chord-form, the bass tone (the chord-5th) is generally doubled.

223. Applied to the first melody of Exercise 16, the result is as follows:

Version 1. All primary chords, and inversions. In every one the root is doubled, excepting in the two $\frac{6}{4}$ chords (doubled bass tone), and in the Dom.-7th chord, where no duplication is necessary. In the last chord, the 5th is omitted, because of the resolution of the leading-tone (7th scale-step) in the Tenor; and therefore the root is tripled.

Version 2. The chord-7th, on the last beat of the first measure, resolves *upward* instead of downward (par. 58, second clause). This is allowed when the bass part moves *in 3rds parallel with it*.

Version 3. Primary and secondary chords. The VI, as usual, harmonizes the first scale-step (in soprano), the II harmonizes the fourth step. In measure 3, second beat, the chord-3rd (*f*-sharp) is doubled,—for the sake of good melodic progressions in the outer parts.

Version 4. More frequent use of the Dom.-7th chord. Compare all four versions *very minutely with each other.*

In all of these versions it will be observed that neither one of the inner voices is distinctly melodious. In the last one, the alto part is undeniably monotonous. This is a condition which can scarcely be avoided by the beginner, and need give him no concern, at present.

Review par. 184, and transpose the above examples to *D minor*.

224. When successive 6ths are used (as in Ex. 132) care must be taken to avoid parallel movement in 5ths or 8ves, between any two parts. Thus:

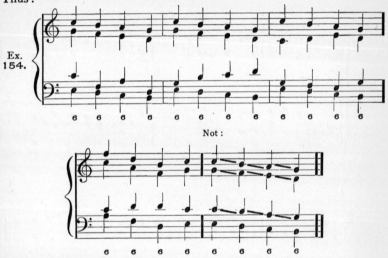

Also in D minor.

225. Sequences are somewhat more difficult, with four parts, because the greater body of tone is less flexible. But they are possible, if planned carefully, according to par. 183. For illustration:

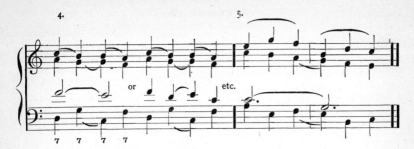

Here again, as in Ex. 133, observe how each sequence *interlocks with the preceding figure,* — as shown by the lower slurs.

226. The so-called Organ-point is particularly valuable in harmony for four (or more) parts, because it adds a line, — *usually the lowermost,* — without interfering with the movements of the other parts.   The principal rule is that the organ-point, as *dissonant* interval, should neither enter nor progress with a leap.   For example (applied to the 7th Melody of Exercise 16):

    1. Organ-point on the Tonic.

Ex. 156.

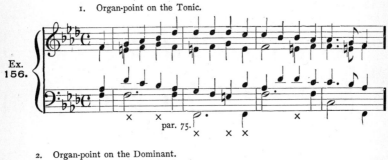

  2. Organ-point on the Dominant.

The ✕ marks the beats where the sustained tone in bass becomes dissonant. In version 1, it is the Tonic of the key; in version 2, the Dominant. No other steps than these are likely to occur as organ-points.

In version 2 there is a raised 6th scale-step in Alto in measure 3, beat 1; and a raised 4th step in measure 4, beat 1.

EXERCISE 22.

FOUR HARMONIC PARTS.   PRIMARY AND SECONDARY CHORDS.   SEQUENCES.

Harmonize, again, all the Melodies given in Exercise 16 and Exercise 17, in four-part harmony, according to the above directions.   This should be done *without reference to the former solutions.*   Do this without fail.

Also write a number of original 4-part sentences, with sequences, successive 6ths, and Organ-points.

CHAPTER XXIII.

MODULATIONS.

227.   All former rules for the changes of key are here again applied, without modification.

Review par. 185 and par. 186.

Melody No. 2 of Exercise 18 may be harmonized as follows in four-voice texture :

Ex. 136.

228   Review par. 188, and pars. 88, 89 and 90.   Besides the chromatic progressions there shown ; — from a triad into a Dom.-7th or diminished-7th chord ; and the chromatic succession of 6ths ; — it is quite common, in four-part harmony, to use a *chromatic succession of diminished-7th chords.*   These movements are all exhibited in the following :

In example *a* there are three irregular chromatic conditions, known as the Cross-relation. In measure 1, beats 3 and 4, the *d* in Soprano is followed by *d-sharp* in Alto; in measure 2, beats 3 and 4, *c* in Tenor is followed by *c-sharp* in Bass; in measure 3, last beat, the Bass has *f-sharp*, followed by *f* in Tenor. When the chromatic succession is thus divided between two different parts, it is simply necessary that the *first of the two chromatic tones should move stepwise*, — not with a leap.

Observe that in example *c* the line of diminished 7ths is always ultimately checked by a resolution into the I. Such a return to the normal condition of chord-relationship is absolutely necessary, *and should not be deferred too long.*

229. The pianoforte music of **Chopin** abounds in beautiful and effective chromatic chord-successions, often extending through a complete sentence. The last phrase in Ex. 158 illustrates this. The student is urged to analyze Chopin's pages very comprehensively and thoughtfully, for such experience as he may desire to gain with reference to this particular kind of flexible harmonic movement. At the same time, he must not neglect the equally faithful analysis of Beethoven, Schubert, Mendelssohn, Schumann, — and Wagner.

Further, — a few random extracts from Chopin:

Number 1. The whole passage is in C minor; nowhere is there evidence of an actual change of key, because the tones involved create the impression of unessential passing-notes only. In measure 2, beat 2, the *f-sharp* is a raised 4th step.

Number 2. This passage is so "contrapuntal" in character, that the individual melody-lines cannot in every case be referred to a legitimate chord; only the *chord-forms* are present,—their names are not always definable. This is obvious in measure 3, beat 2. In measure 5, beat 3, the *purpose* is a I of B major; the *a-sharp* in Alto is a passing-note. Similar conditions prevail in Ex. 149, No. 3, the Notes to which should here be reviewed.

Number 3. In measure 2, beat 3, the *g-natural* in Bass is merely a passing-note, which does no more than change the mode of the chord from major to minor (compare Notes to Ex. 149, No. 1). Measure 6 is similar, though here the *c* in Bass is a legitimate lowered 6th step of E major. In measure 4, beat 3,—again similar,— the *e-flat* in Bass is a passing-note only.

Number 4. A succession of Dom.-7th chords, in fundamental form, and, consequently, with persistent parallel 5ths. See par. 107, especially the last clause.

N. B. This paragraph (229), and the above examples, belong properly to the next chapter. It is not the purpose of the present lesson to use any other than essential tones (chord-intervals).

230. For the rules of altered scale-steps; review pars. 190, 191, and 192.

In four-voice harmony their application is as follows, in major:

1. Lowered 6th step.   2. Raised 4th step.

Ex.
160.
C Major.

IV I ₒV⁹ I   II⁷ I IV I IV V⁷

3. Raised 4th and 2nd.   4. Raised 2nd step (in *Dom.*).

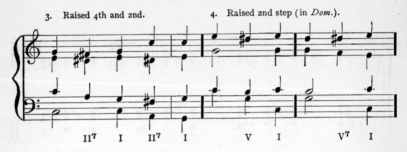

II⁷ I II⁷ I   V I   V⁷ I

5. Lowered 6th and 2nd (in *Major*).

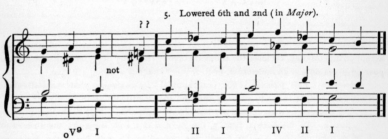

ₒV⁹ I   II I   IV II I

When the 2nd step is raised in the Dom. discords, it should lie *above*, not below, the chord-7th.

Further, in minor:

1. Raised 6th step.   2. Lowered 7th step.   3. Raised 4th step.

Ex.
161.
C Minor.

IV⁷ V I   III IV I   II⁷ I   IV⁷ I

Probably the most common of these are groups 3 and 4.

Observe that here, unlike major, the altered chords do not *always* progress into the I.

EXERCISE 23.

MODULATIONS.

1. Harmonize, again, all the melodies given in Ex. 18, in four-part harmony, according to the above directions. *Do this without fail, and thoroughly.*

2. Harmonize the following melodies:

[A solution of Melody 5 will be found in the Appendix.]

3. Besides these, write a number of original four-voice sentences, with the material of this chapter.

CHAPTER XXIV.

CONTRAPUNTAL HARMONY.

231. Review par. 193, the principle of which is applied to the four-voiced texture also, and in the same manner.

232. In the following example, the given melody is placed in the Soprano. Review par. 194.

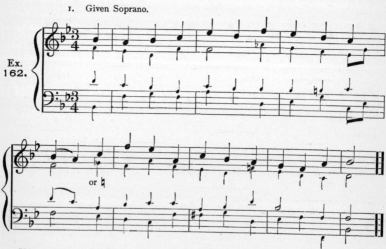

Ex.
162.

Here again, as in Ex. 140, there is significant evidence of fundamental agreement between the *two outer parts*,—as if, unconsciously, the Bass were counterpointed to the Soprano alone, with more reference to general melodic agreement than to the chords. It is probable that this is always preponderantly the case, in music of every kind; for both outer parts, because of their prominence, are melodic leaders; and their good contrapuntal association guarantees the complete harmonious result, into which the two inner parts necessarily fall.

This attaches a degree of importance to the Bass (or lowermost part), which the student is warned not to underrate, or overlook.

Observe the movements of the lowermost part in many sentences in **Beethoven, Mendelssohn** and others. See the 5th Waltz of **Chopin** (A-flat, op. 42), measures 29–41 from the end.

233. Review, very thoroughly, pars. 197, 198 and 199. The above simple harmonic version may be amplified to a constant rhythm of two notes to a beat, in alternating parts, about as follows:

Ex. 163.

Compare this very carefully with the original form (Ex. 162).

Observe, here again, that the quicker rhythm is applied, in the *upper part*, to the unaccented beats, — with one exception, in the first measure.

234. Review par. 195. — In four-voice harmony, the given melody cannot conveniently be used in the same key for each of the four parts.

A given Soprano is placed one octave lower for the Tenor; and a given Bass, one octave higher for the Alto. The given Soprano is transposed either a 4th or 5th downward for the Alto; and the given Bass a 4th or 5th upward for the Tenor. For example, if the given Melody is in C, the keys will be as follows:

Soprano — C
Alto — G or F
Tenor — C
Bass — G or F.

The above given Soprano (Ex. 162, B-flat major) may therefore be placed in F major for the Alto.   Thus:

2.   Given Alto (transposed).

Ex. 164.

Here, the *Bass* agrees contrapuntally with the given Alto, as if these two parts were unconsciously conceived together.   Note the parallel 3ds in meas. 3.

235.   This may be amplified to a constant rhythm of three notes to each beat, in alternating parts, about as follows:

Ex. 165.

Compare minutely with the original model, Ex. 164.   Observe, again, the treatment of the rhythm in the upper part.

236. Review par. 196. — For the Bass voice, a new Melody is here chosen, for greater variety of illustration :

Here the agreement of the Soprano with the given Bass is conspicuous. Compare the Notes to Ex. 162.   As to the monotony and meagre melodic contents of the Tenor, review the Notes to Ex. 153, version 4 ; — and observe how, in the amplified form (Ex. 167), this Tenor becomes as melodious as the other parts.

237. This simple harmonic sentence may be amplified, about as follows, to a rhythm of four notes to each beat :

Compare carefully with Ex. 166.

238. The above given Bass (Ex. 166, *E* minor) may be placed in *B* minor for the Tenor:

4.   Given Tenor (transposed).

Ex.
168.

Here, both the Soprano and the Bass, — separately, — harmonize admirably with the given Tenor.

It is probably unwise to lay too much stress upon these harmonious results, with reference to any particular part or parts, because they are no doubt nothing more than the natural consequences of choosing the correct chords.   At the same time, if the student finds that the intentional adoption of such a process facilitates the task of harmonization, he may be sure that it is a perfectly legitimate mode of procedure. And, at all events, he must carefully guard the principle dictated in the Notes to Ex. 162, *and always provide for a good, melodious lowermost part.*

239. The above harmonic phrase (Ex. 168) may be amplified to a constant rhythm of four notes to each group, as follows:

Ex.
169.

Compare minutely with Ex. 168, — not only as a whole, but *each part separately.*

In the second version of measures 3 and 4, the *c-natural* in Tenor is used as lowered 2nd scale-step (of *b* minor); in anticipation of this legitimate "alteration," the whole harmonic current sets into C major. The *f-sharp* in Soprano is a little harsh, but inevitable, as it is the very means of establishing *b* minor, and proving the identity of *c* as lowered 2nd step.

EXERCISE 24.

CONTRAPUNTAL FOUR-PART HARMONY.

1. Amplify Ex. 162 also to a constant rhythm of 3 notes to each beat, in alternating parts; and then to 4-note groups.
   Amplify Ex. 164, similarly, to 2-note groups; and to 4-note groups.
   Amplify Ex. 166 to 2-note groups; and to 3-note groups.
   Amplify Ex. 168 to 2-note groups; and to 3-note groups.

2. Place the given melody of Ex. 162 also in the *Tenor*, in *A* major. And also in the *Bass*, in *E* major. Each version thus obtained is to be amplified as usual to 2-note groups, 3-note groups, and 4-note groups.

Place the given melody of Ex. 166 also in the Soprano, in *a* minor; and also
in the Alto, in *d* minor.   Each version thus obtained is to be amplified to
2-note, 3-note, and 4-note groups.

3. Harmonize each of the following given melodies in the four ways exhibited
above; first as Soprano; then as Tenor (in the same key, an octave lower); then as
Alto, a 4th or 5th lower than where it is written; and then as Bass, in the same key
as the Alto version, one octave lower:

Each version thus obtained is to be amplified as usual to 2-note, 3-note, and
4-note groups; — each melody must yield 16 different solutions.

This task presents peculiar difficulties, and the student must undertake it with
patience and faithful persistence.   A partial solution of each will be found in the
Appendix, to which he may refer *after* having exhausted his own ingenuity upon
them.   Those given versions, also, are to be amplified as usual.

4. Manipulate, *at the keyboard*, each one of the above simple harmonic versions
(including Exs. 162, 164, 166 and 168) in a rhythm of *two notes to each beat, with shifted
parts* (syncopation), as shown in Ex. 144, B.

CHAPTER XXV.

FOUR-PART COUNTERPOINT.

240.   Review, very thoroughly, par. 204.   Also par. 205; and par.
206; and par. 207.

241.   The devices explained in par. 206, — parallel 3rds and 6ths, and
"opposite duplication," — are here again, in four-part counterpoint,

convenient and valuable; especially in what must still be regarded as *elementary* contrapuntal exercises.

Review Exs. 147 and 148 ; and see the following:

The "parallel 3rds and 6ths" are indicated by dashes; the "opposite duplications," by slurs.

Again the student is reminded that these devices are useful and legitimate in *elementary* counterpoint, but by no means characteristic of the higher grades of polyphonic writing. They serve, sometimes admirably, to sustain the rhythmic momentum of the parts, — especially, as has been seen, during the necessary prolongation of a chord; and often tend to overcome easily and smoothly some harmonic embarrassment.

242. As for the more serious details of four-part counterpoint, the student can find no surer means of increasing his knowledge and experience than *the careful study and analysis of good contrapuntal models*.

In pursuing this method of training, he should adopt the method indicated in the following analytical exercises. Thus: First define the chords, by the *letters* which they contain, and also, as far as possible, by *name* in their key; then define the unessential (passing and neighboring) tones; and carefully note all the linear details, — sequences, imitations, and other evidences of purpose and agreement in the formation and arrangement of the *melodic figures*. For illustration:

No. 1.   BACH, Organ fugue in C minor.

Ex. 171.

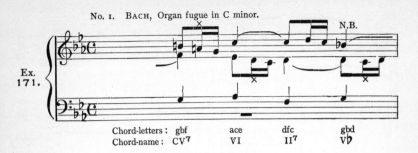

Chord-letters :	gbf	ace	dfc	gbd
Chord-name :	CV⁷	VI	II⁷	V♮

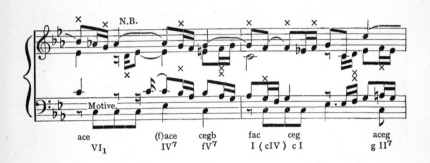

	ace		(f)ace	cegb	fac	ceg		aceg
	VI₁		IV⁷	fV⁷	I (cIV) c I			g II⁷

dfac	gbd		aceg		dfa		gbd
V⁷	I		II⁷		V		GI

No. 2.   BACH, Organ fugue in B minor.

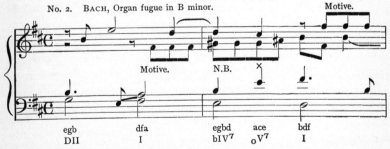

egb	dfa	egbd	ace	bdf
DII	I	bIV⁷	ₒV⁷	I

No. 3. Mozart, "Requiem."

No. 4. Mendelssohn, Pianoforte Fugue in E minor.

No. 5. MENDELSSOHN, Pianoforte Fugue in D major.

No. 7. BRAHMS, German Requiem.

Every inharmonic tone is marked **x**, throughout all these numbers. The tones not thus marked form the chord, whose letters (and name) are given beneath.

Observe, throughout, that the chords represent either tonic, dominant or subdominant harmony; that the dominant almost invariably moves into the I (or VI) of its key; and that the subdominant (IV or II) usually moves into the dominant. In other words, *observe the prevalence of the progression* **II-V7-I**, and compare par. 169, — also pars. 174 and 175.

Besides these general traits, observe the following details:

In No. 1 : Measure 1, beat 4, the *b-flat* in Soprano is the lowered 7th scale-step, on the way down. In measure 2, beat 2, the manner in which the three **upper** voices coöperate to carry on the four 16ths of the beat.

In No. 2 : Measure 2, beat 1, the *g-sharp* in the Alto is the raised 6th step, on the way up. Notice, particularly, the descending scale in Bass (in half-notes), and how this line is later imitated in Alto, and, syncopated, in Soprano and Tenor. In measure 4, the *a* in Soprano is the lowered 7th step of B minor, used on the way down, in preparation (also) of E major.

In No. 3 : Measure 3½, beat 2, the *c-sharp* in Tenor is the raised 4th step.

In No. 5 : Measure 2 is, strictly speaking, all dominant harmony, although the fourth 8th-note *sounds* like a brief tonic. Similar long dominant chords are found in No. 7, near beginning and end. Compare paragraph 207 (Ex. 148, No. 4).

In No. 6 : At the beginning there is a succession of Sixth-chords, over the tonic organ-point. Compare paragraph 182 (Ex. 132).

EXERCISE 25.

ANALYSIS.

Analyze, similarly, each of the following extracts, in the given order. Determine the *chord-letters*, as shown in the above example; and mark all inharmonic tones. *This is the most important detail of the analysis.* The chord-*names* may be added, wherever they appear definable. Also note, particularly, all the linear details, and the relation of the figures and tone-lines to each other, — with reference, for instance, to par. 206 (Ex. 147).

[The student may need to be cautioned against being over-scrupulous. It is not necessary to define every tone. He should learn to analyze, at first, somewhat superficially; first defining those chord-forms (and chord-names) that are quite evident, and adding minuter definitions as the passage assumes a clearer *general* character in his mind. Above all things, he should recollect that, in counterpoint, the TONE-LINES are of paramount importance.]

    Bach, " Well-tempered Clavichord " : —

Volume I, Fugue   No.   5 (D major), measure 5, to the end.

   "   " Prelude No. 12 (F minor), measure 11, to the end.

   "   " Fugue   No. 16 (G minor), measure 15 to 18.

   "   " Prelude No.   7 (E♭ major), measure 1 to 4; 10 to 25; 32 to 41: 58, to the end.

   "   " Fugue   No. 12 (F minor), last 6 measures.

   "   " Fugue   No. 14 (F♯ minor), last 9 measures.

   "   " Fugue   No. 18 (G♯ minor), measure 7 to 11.

   "   " Fugue   No. 20 (A minor), measure 11 to 15.

"   " Fugue No. 23 (B major), measure 12 to 18.
"   " Fugue No.   1 (C major), measure 5 to 7; 16 to 19; 22, to the end.
Volume II, Prelude No.   1 (C major), measure 11 to 20.
"   " Fugue No.   7 (E♭ major), measure 21 to 30; 58, to the end.
"   " Fugue No.   9 (E major), measure 5, to the end.
"   " Fugue No. 16 (G minor), measure 51 to 67.
"   " Fugue No.   2 (C minor), measure 19, to the end.
"   " Fugue No. 23 (B major), measure 19 to 27; last 12 measures.
"   " Fugue No. 22 (B♭ minor), measure 17 to 25; 42 to 46.
"   " Fugue No.   8 (D♯ minor), last 6 measures.
"   " Fugue No.   5 (D major), measures 10 to 16; 24, to the end.

After finishing these, the student may analyze any example of 4-part counter-point that he may find, in the works of Bach, Händel, Mendelssohn, Rheinberger and other modern writers.

CHAPTER XXVI.

MOTIVE-DEVELOPMENT.

243. Review pars. 142 to 145. Also pars. 212, 213, 214, 215 and 216. These all have bearing upon four-part counterpoint, also.

244. The rule given in par. 217 should be applied with still greater emphasis to a contrapuntal sentence with four parts. At least one of the parts should be restrained in its movements, — that is, heavier (longer) tones should occur frequently in one and another of the parts, in contrast with the prevailing quicker rhythm. This may be seen, to some extent, in Ex. 170.

Further, *rests* should be frequently introduced; not only brief ones; whole groups of beats should be silent now and then in one, and then another, of the parts, — so that while four parts are unquestionably represented, they are not always active together. In this manner, the student's task is reduced for a part of the time to three-part counterpoint, and the result is all the more effective.

245. The development of a Motive with four contrapuntal parts, while subject to all the general conditions of foregoing chapters, requires a somewhat more definite system of announcement and imitation, *at the beginning.* The following schedule must be adopted:

    1. The Motive may first appear in any one of the four parts. And, if need be, a few intermediate tones may be added, with strict regard to pars. 213 and 214.

2. The second announcement (first Imitation) must appear in the *next higher or next lower* part, — in the Dominant key (compare par. 212).

3. The third announcement must be in the original key, *one octave lower or higher* than the *first* announcement. and therefore in a " parallel " part of the latter.

4. The fourth announcement must be *one octave lower or higher* than the *second* one, — again in the Dominant key.   This will always be the last one of the four parts, the one which has remained unused.

Between each of these announcements brief episodes may be introduced, if necessary.

For example, with the first Motive of Exercise 21 :

Episode : Mod. to C.

M. in Bass (Dom. key).

Episode : Mod. to Subdom. and to orig. key.

d V⁷_____ D I   =   g V_____

molto rall.   (b)

I = F II   F V_____I   (bb min.)   F maj.

molto rall.

or :   Motive.

F I   II⁷   V⁷   I

Analyze this (first without, and then with, the keyboard) most thoroughly. Observe that the counterpoint does not become "four-part" until the last part announces the Motive (measure 10). The four parts are then retained steadily to the end, excepting one measure rest in the Alto. This is somewhat contrary to the spirit of paragraph 244, but cannot be wrong, of course.

In the second version of the ending, one additional announcement of the Motive is made, in the Tenor. The *d-flat* (in Alto) is, in both cases, practically the lowered 6th scale-step of F major.

246. The above sentence is much shorter than any of the Inventions with two voices, or with three voices, made in Exercises 15 and 21. Should a more extended form be desirable, the schedule given in par. 154 may be consulted, but will probably be utilized more as a general guide, than literally. Compare par. 219.

EXERCISE 26.

MOTIVE-DEVELOPMENT, WITH FOUR CONTRAPUNTAL PARTS.

1. Make three more complete solutions of the Motive manipulated in Ex. 172, *beginning with Soprano* (in same key); *then beginning with Bass* (C or B major); *and then with Alto* (C or B major).

2. Manipulate each of the following Motives, in the manner above suggested. Each Motive may be developed in four wholly different ways, by placing the first announcement respectively in each of the four parts (in different keys, — as indicated above, and according to the suggestions given in par. 234). Review all the directions in Exercise 21, No. 3.

1. Alto or Bass. (Sopr. or Tenor, in *A♭*.)

2. Bass or Alto. (Tenor or Sopr., in *e*.)

3. Tenor or Sopr. (Bass or Alto, in *A*.)

4. Sopr. or Tenor. (Alto or Bass, in *c♯*.)

5. Sopr. or Tenor. (Alto or Bass, in *E.*)

[A concise solution of Motive 5 will be found in the Appendix.]

3. Besides these, manipulate again (with four parts) some of the Motives given in Exercise 15 and in Exercise 21, — subject to pars. 213 and 214, if needed.

4. Further, the student may invent a number of original Motives, similar to the above, and manipulate them in the usual manner.

*   *   *

This is as far as the study of Elementary Counterpoint need extend. For the continuation of his contrapuntal discipline, the student may take up the author's *Applied Counterpoint*, beginning with Chapter IV.

But before doing so, or in systematic alternation with the latter, he is urgently advised to pursue a thorough course in free composition, as detailed in the author's *Homophonic Forms*.

*   *   *

The End.

APPENDIX.

SOLUTIONS OF SOME OF THE GIVEN EXERCISES.

a. As upper part.

Exercise 9,
Melody 4.

pars. 48 and 184.

b. As lower part.

a. As upper part.

Exercise 11,
Melody 3.

b. As lower part.

(Accelerated.)

a. As upper part.

Exercise 12,
Melody 2.

a. As upper part.   Susp.

Exercise 19,
Melody 3.

(Amplified to 2-tone groups)

b.   As inner part.

II   II⁷

(Amplified to 3-tone groups)

3

3

II   II⁷

b. As lower part.

IV (II)

(Amplified to 4-tone groups)

II⁷

No. 1. Upper part given.

Exercise 20.

Motive.

(" Intentional " 8ves.)

Motive. *molto rit.* *Adagio.*

Exercise 23, Melody 5.

b. The given melody as Tenor part.

Exercise 24,
Melody 1.

or :   f II⁷

c. As Alto part (transposed.)

Notes to
Ex. 158a.

V⁷   I E♭V⁷_____I

par. 14.

b. The given melody as Tenor part.

Exercise 24,
Melody 2.

Ex. 158a.

d. As Bass part (transposed).

or : etc.

b. The given melody as Tenor part.

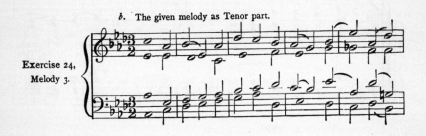

Exercise 24,
Melody 3.

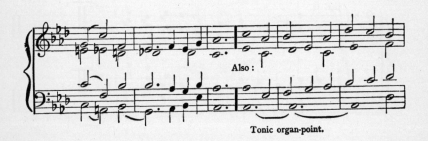

Also :

Tonic organ-point.

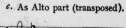

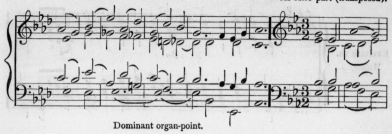

Dominant organ-point.

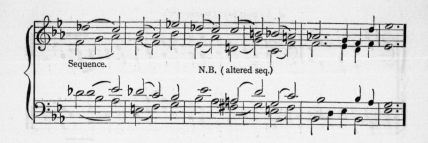

Sequence.   N.B. (altered seq.)

d.   As Bass part (transposed).

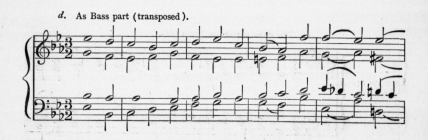

Each of these versions of Exercise 24 is to be amplified, in the usual manner, to 2-note, 3-note, and 4-note groups.

Exercise 26,
Motive 5.

AURAL HARMONY

Part I

FRANKLIN W. ROBINSON

LONG a teacher of harmony, the author had come to feel an intense need for its presentation in a form that would seek to appeal to one's musical consciousness through the ear, and thus afford the power to hear what is written. This work is the result of his conclusions. At the end of a most illuminating preface, in which are treated the aspects of Physics, Physiology and Psychology and their relation to harmony-study, the inductive is chosen as the legitimate method of approach in a treatise on aural harmony, and the presentation proceeds accordingly. The work proper is divided into fifteen chapters. Opening with an analytical exposition of the Scale, it traverses all of the intermediary study features of its subject up to the Secondary Triads in Minor, with certain related inversions, and there it rests. The aural principle is maintained throughout, and each chapter concludes with a special, often illustrated, division called "aural practice." Nobody can gainsay the logic and appeal of this unique book, nor deny its need among harmony students.

New York · G. SCHIRMER · Boston

A 590

ETHICS *and* ESTHETICS
of PIANO-PLAYING
By Constantin von Sternberg

THE author emphasizes chiefly the esthetic aspect of piano-playing, "the lucid demonstration on the piano of thematic design." He suggests ways to conceive a musical thought intelligently and to convey it clearly through skilful phrasing. The importance of phrasing is emphasized and its two essential elements, pause and accent, are fully treated. There is an illuminating discussion of the Art-pause and its usefulness in expressing the inner content of music. Accent, the sole means of conveying rhythm, "the handle by which the auditor grasps music," is taken up in a thoroughly practical fashion. The book will prove invaluable to the teacher who wishes to keep pace with new musical ideas; to the student who strives for more than mere technical skill; and to the artist who represents in the highest degree the ethical and esthetic aspects of piano-playing.

New York · G. SCHIRMER · Boston

A 600

DATE DUE

MAY 1 5 2005			